PERSUASION
a screenplay

Nick Dear's many theatre credits include *The Art of Success* for the Royal Shakespeare Company and subsequently Manhattan Theatre Club, New York. It won him the 1986 John Whiting Award and was nominated for an Olivier Award. Other plays include *Temptation* (RSC, 1984), *Pure Science* (RSC, 1986), *A Family Affair* (after Ostrovsky; Cheek by Jowl, 1988 – Olivier Award nomination), *In the Ruins* (Bristol Old Vic/Royal Court, 1990), *The Last Days of Don Juan* (after Tirso de Molina; RSC, 1990), *Le Bourgeois Gentilhomme* (after Molière; RNT, 1992), *Zenobia* (RSC, 1995). He has also collaborated with Peter Brook on the development of *Qui est là?* (Bouffes du Nord, 1996). *Persuasion*, his first feature film screenplay, was shown on BBC Television in 1995, and subsequently released in cinemas worldwide. It won five BAFTA Awards including Best Single Drama, and the Broadcasting Press Guild Award. He has since co-authored a film based on Dostoyevsky's *The Gambler*.

new and forthcoming titles in the Methuen Film series

Beautiful Thing
Jonathan Harvey

The Crucible
Arthur Miller

Twelfth Night
Trevor Nunn after Shakespeare

The Krays
Philip Ridley

The Reflecting Skin & The Passion of Darkly Noon
Philip Ridley

The English Patient
Anthony Minghella

for a complete catalogue of Methuen Drama titles write to:

Methuen Drama
Michelin House
81 Fulham Road
London SW3 6RB

PERSUASION

by Jane Austen

a screenplay by
Nick Dear

Methuen Film

A METHUEN SCREENPLAY

First published in Great Britain in 1996
by Methuen Drama
an imprint of Reed International Books Ltd
Michelin House, 81 Fulham Road, London SW3 6RB
and distributed in the United States of America
by Heinemann, a division of Reed Elsevier Inc
361 Hanover Street, Portsmouth, New Hampshire NH 03901 3959

A CIP catalogue record for this book
is available from the British Library

ISBN 0 413 71170 6

Typeset in 10 on 13.5 point Plantin Light
by Wilmaset Ltd, Birkenhead, Wirral
Printed in Great Britain
by Cox & Wyman Ltd, Reading, Berkshire

PERSUASION

INTRODUCTION

PERSUASION IS A LOVE STORY. Normally I run a mile from such things. As my son would say, 'All that girlie business.' I tried to make *Persuasion* more palatable to his six-year-old taste by not putting any kissing in it – 'kissing! ugh!' – but in the end greater minds than mine decreed that you can't have a love story without kissing in it. Well, perhaps you can't. Hard luck, Finn.

There are reasons, though, why this particular girlie business attracted me, where other girlie business – the Hollywood variety – tends to leave me frothing at the mouth (and quite unkissable). It's a love story in the Cinderella mould, which is played out with few major surprises, and happily resolved. Superficially, that's all. But when I read it I was struck by the realism, the truthfulness, of Austen's depiction of two people who fall in love, part, and are then reunited. No author, to my mind, has done it better. And anybody who's been lucky enough to have loved and been loved in return, I thought – especially those of us who've had a bit of a wait – will identify with this. It's an expression of something which binds people together across the world, and it's worth restating once in a while. Most popular films pander to our worst instincts, their endless barbarism very clearly confluent with the recent foul massacres in Dunblane and Tasmania. In Austen we find the opposite: an invitation to discover the best of ourselves, and to celebrate what little greatness we might be capable of in our tiny lives.

For aeons it's been deeply unfashionable for art to try and deal with these matters. As Edward Bond declaimed, 'I write about violence as naturally as Jane Austen wrote about manners.' And this rather patronising put-down usefully characterises what Austen's work has long been thought to be about. Elegant drawing-rooms, frilly cuffs, confidences exchanged over cups of tea – all very English, very antique, very *dead*. Why then has it suddenly sprung to life? Because true love is a common currency, and restraint, and devotion, and not-forgetting, are qualities we rightly admire whatever our situation. You can be in love if you're fighting a battle; you can be in love if you have no shoes. The idiosyncracies of the human heart are too often ignored by our ideologues.

Bond's remark opened his preface to *Lear*, a great play. A play which uses gross physical violence as a metaphor for the political inequities of a society governed by systems of class. But Austen utilises 'manners' – at least in *Persuasion* – to exactly the same purpose. The story essentially describes an old order fading away into decadence, and a new tribe, a meritocracy, coming to the fore. In other words, it marks the turning point between the eighteenth century and the nineteenth. Yes, it's still the old girlie business, but it's also about a world in transition, and that caught my attention. Something else is going on. The romance doesn't take place in a vacuum, but within an organically evolving society. There's an undertow of political reality which makes the syrup a little less sweet.

Of course it's still a very sour mouthful for the style police to have to swallow. Love after Hiroshima? Get real. In today's world, you wear your cynicism like a suit of armour. 'Get real', the sign-off phrase of the twentieth century, roughly translating as: 'You're an innocent. I know about life, and it sucks. Expect to get shafted, and treat people accordingly.' But is that really our experience? Don't most of us fall in love, or hope to? Don't most of us find partners and settle down, or try to? Or keep trying to, and failing, and trying again? This isn't being romantic. This is getting real. It's a real book, and I like it.

Nick Dear, June 1996

CAST

ANNE ELLIOT	Amanda Root
CAPTAIN WENTWORTH	Ciaran Hinds
LADY RUSSELL	Susan Fleetwood
SIR WALTER ELLIOT	Corin Redgrave
MRS CROFT	Fiona Shaw
ADMIRAL CROFT	John Woodvine
ELIZABETH ELLIOT	Phoebe Nicholls
MR ELLIOT	Samuel West
MARY MUSGROVE	Sophie Thompson
MRS MUSGROVE	Judy Cornwell
CHARLES MUSGROVE	Simon Russell Beale
MRS CLAY	Felicity Dean
MR MUSGROVE	Roger Hammond
LOUISA MUSGROVE	Emma Roberts
HENRIETTA MUSGROVE	Victoria Hamilton
CAPTAIN HARVILLE	Robert Glenister
CAPTAIN BENWICK	Richard McCabe
MRS SMITH	Helen Schlesinger
NURSE ROOKE	Jane Wood
MR SHEPHERD	David Collings
LADY DALRYMPLE	Darlene Johnson
MISS CARTERET	Cinnamon Faye
HENRY HAYTER	Isaac Maxwell-Hunt
SIR HENRY WILLOUGHBY	Roger Llewellyn
MRS HARVILLE	Sally George
NAVAL OFFICERS	David Acton
	Justin Avoth
JEMIMA	Lonnie James
LANDLORD	Roger Watkins
APOTHECARY	David Plummer
COACHMAN	Richard Bremmer
TRADESMEN	Bill McGuirk
	Niall Refoy
LADY DALRYMPLE'S BUTLER	Ken Shorter
FOOTMAN	Dermot Kerrigan
LITTLE CHARLES	Tom Rigby
LITTLE WALTER	Alex Wilman
CONCERT OPERA SINGER	Rosa Mannion

Executive Producer BBC-TV	George Faber
Executive Producer WGBH/Boston	Rebecca Eaton
Producer	Fiona Finlay
Director	Roger Michell
Make-up Designer	Jean Speak
Costume Designer	Alexandra Byrne
Original Music	Jeremy Sams
Film Editor	Kate Evans
Designers	William Dudley and Brian Sykes
Director of Photography	John Daly

A BBC production in association with WGBH/Boston and Millésime/France 2

THE OCEAN. DAY.
From underwater, a line of oars cut into a choppy sea, in perfect rhythm.

OVERLOOKING KELLYNCH. DAY.
Somerset, 1814. Early September. A one-horse gig clatters through the lush landscape carrying SHEPHERD, *a market-town lawyer, and his daughter* MRS CLAY. *As it drives over the brow of a hill the substantial country seat known as Kellynch Hall comes into view below them.* MRS CLAY *smiles; but* SHEPHERD *bites his lip, looking worried.*

THE OCEAN. DAY.
The oars belong to a ten-oar cutter. A crew of burly sailors rows it towards a ship-of-the-line which is riding at anchor in the distance. In the stern of the cutter sits ADMIRAL CROFT, *in full dress uniform, well-balanced against the roll of the boat, his eye fixed on the warship.*

KELLYNCH PARK. DAY.
SHEPHERD's *gig passes through the park on its way to the Hall.* MRS CLAY *admires the setting. She is not pretty, but she is youthful and bright, with an excellent figure. Her face is distinctive, with a mass of freckles and a protruding tooth.*

WARSHIP. DAY.

The ADMIRAL*'s cutter comes alongside the warship, and a ladder is let down. The ship's crew are lined up along the rails. The officers cluster round the head of the ladder as the* ADMIRAL *ascends.*

KELLYNCH. DAY.

SHEPHERD *halts his gig at the stairs leading up to the grand front door of Kellynch Hall.* TWO GROOMS *in livery instantly appear. They hold the horse, whilst the occupants disembark. The* BUTLER *and the* UNDER-BUTLER *emerge from the front door. Even for such a large house, the number of staff is excessive.*

As SHEPHERD, *with* MRS CLAY *on his arm, and clutching his portmanteau, reaches the steps, several* TRADESMEN *who have been waiting there surround him, waving bills and documents. Both they and* SHEPHERD *speak with a West Country burr.*

TRADESMAN 1: Mr Shepherd –
TRADESMAN 2: When are we to be paid?
SHEPHERD: In due course.
TRADESMAN 1 (*waving bills*): But these are outstanding.
    But SHEPHERD *has pushed through and now makes his way up the stairs to the door. The* UNDER-BUTLER *attempts to hold back the* TRADESMEN.

WARSHIP. DAY.

Camera runs along the faces of the ragged crew as the ADMIRAL *boards the warship. Some of the crew look pleased, some apprehensive: a pretty desperate lot, hardened from years at sea. The officers salute their* ADMIRAL.

2

KELLYNCH. DAY.

As SHEPHERD *and* MRS CLAY *enter the house, we see* LADY RUSSELL*'s carriage pull up behind theirs, and the footmen running with a stool to assist her out.*

STATEROOM. DAY.

ADMIRAL CROFT *is in the ship's stateroom with a full complement of officers. They are a good-looking and congenial set of men. A* STEWARD *passes among them with a tray of drinks.*

ADMIRAL: Gentlemen. The war is over.
  General pleasure.
OFFICER: And Bonaparte, sir?
ADMIRAL: Bonaparte has abdicated. He's confined to the island of Elba. We're going home.
COMMODORE: Gentlemen: the Admiral.
  They raise their glasses in a toast to ADMIRAL CROFT.
OFFICERS: The Admiral!

KELLYNCH – DRAWING-ROOM. DAY.

SIR WALTER ELLIOT: No. I will not have a sailor in my house. I strongly object to the Navy.
  A crisis meeting is in progress in the Kellynch drawing-room, presided over by SIR WALTER ELLIOT. *He is a vain man, but still handsome – exquisitely dressed and coiffeured. He and* SHEPHERD *stand; the ladies sit. Present with* LADY RUSSELL *and* MRS CLAY *is* SIR WALTER*'s daughter,* ELIZABETH. *She's twenty-nine, and accustomed to large quantities of luxury. She reclines in front of the fire, munching sweetmeats. Although the logs burn strongly in the grate, one small Regency fireplace is hardly enough to heat this vast, high-ceilinged space. So*

3

visitors always feel a chill in the drawing-room. SIR
WALTER *is used to having his say, at length, on any
subject. He considers himself the very pinnacle of wit.*

SIR WALTER: It brings persons of obscure birth into undue
distinction; and it cuts up a man's youth and vigour
most horribly. One day last spring, in town, I was in
company with a certain Admiral Baldwin, the most
deplorable looking personage you can imagine, his face
the colour of mahogany, rough and rugged, all lines and
wrinkles, with nine grey hairs along the side, and
nothing but a dab of powder on the top. 'In the name of
heaven, who is that old fellow?' said I to Sir Basil
Morley, who was standing near. 'Old fellow!' cried Sir
Basil, 'that is Admiral Baldwin, who is forty, and no
more!' And it is the same with them all. They are
knocked about, and exposed to every climate, and every
weather, until they are not fit to be seen in society.

MRS CLAY: Have a little mercy on the poor men, Sir Walter!
We were not all born to be handsome.

SIR WALTER *revels in the flattery. He gives* MRS CLAY
his most winning smile.

SHEPHERD: You will not have a naval man as a tenant?

SIR WALTER: I will not, Shepherd, no.

SHEPHERD: Then there is but one course open to you. You
must retrench.

SIR WALTER: Retrench?

ELIZABETH: Retrench . . . ?

SIR WALTER: How may I retrench? A Baronet must be seen
to live like a Baronet!

ELIZABETH *nods her agreement. She doesn't like*
SHEPHERD, *though* MRS CLAY *is her special friend.*
SHEPHERD *looks pointedly to* LADY RUSSELL, *who
produces a document. She is of similar age to* SIR
WALTER.

LADY RUSSELL: Sir Walter, I have been your neighbour for a good many years, and I am as solicitous for the credit of your family as any body could well be. But your debts are extreme. You must retrench. I have, therefore, taken the liberty of drawing up some plans of economy for your household. I have made exact calculations, and I have consulted Anne on some points of detail.

ELIZABETH: Anne? Why?

At that moment SIR WALTER's *second daughter,* ANNE, *slips into the room. She carries a large bunch of keys, and is flushed from hurrying to attend to her jobs around the house before coming to the meeting.* ANNE *is dressed very much more plainly than* ELIZABETH, *and although in fact a couple of years younger, looks the older of the two. She takes a seat in the corner, away from the fire.* LADY RUSSELL *smiles at* ANNE *and hands her document to* SIR WALTER. SIR WALTER *splutters as he reads the recommendations. He puffs out his cheeks and very nearly stamps his well-shod foot.*

SIR WALTER: What! Every comfort of life knocked off! Journeys, London, servants, table – !

He passes the paper to ELIZABETH, *who, after one quick look, throws it aside.* SIR WALTER *gestures up at the paintings of horses and dogs which hang on the walls. The rings on his fingers sparkle.*

SIR WALTER: I had sooner quit Kellynch Hall at once, than remain in it on such disgraceful terms!

KELLYNCH – DINING-ROOM. DAY.
The party takes luncheon. They are being served an exquisite iced sorbet, which has been sculpted in the shape of a swan. The atmosphere has become more reasonable . . .

SHEPHERD (*to* SIR WALTER): Bath is but fifty mile from Kellynch, and, if I may be permitted my opinion, altogether a safer location for a gentleman in your predicament. In Bath, I think, you may be important at comparatively little expense.

MRS CLAY (*to* ELIZABETH): Sorbet in September! How delightful.

ELIZABETH (*to* MRS CLAY): Enjoy it, for there will be no more ice until the winter.

LADY RUSSELL (*to* SIR WALTER): Bath is most congenial. The new Assembly Rooms are splendid; there are concerts and recitals every week.

SIR WALTER *looks thoughtful.*

SIR WALTER: I am for Bath. I have always said Bath is incomparable.

KELLYNCH – DRAWING-ROOM. DAY.
The party are back in the drawing-room, where the meeting began. They are taking afternoon tea and cakes. SIR WALTER *stands at the window, peering out glumly at his estate.*

SIR WALTER: . . . Who is this Admiral Croft?

SHEPHERD: I met with him at the Quarter Sessions in Taunton. He is a native of Somersetshire, who has acquired a very handsome fortune in the war, and wishes to return here.

SIR WALTER: Yes, but who *is* he?

ANNE *looks a little pale.* LADY RUSSELL *glances at her, and continues to watch her closely.*

ANNE: He is a Rear Admiral of the White. He was in the Trafalgar action, and has been in the East Indies since. He has been stationed there, I believe, several years.

SIR WALTER: Then I take it for granted that his face has both the colour and texture of this macaroon.

SIR WALTER *laughs at his wit, accompanied by* MRS CLAY. *He returns to his customary place in front of the fire, one elbow geometrically positioned on the mantelpiece, the other hand tucked into the velveteen pocket of his waistcoat.*

SHEPHERD: The Admiral is a little weather-beaten, to be sure, but not much. He is a married man, but without children. A house is never taken care of, Sir Walter, without a lady, and a lady with no children is the very best preserver of furniture in the world. Moreover, I found that Mrs Croft is herself not unconnected in this country.

SIR WALTER: Oh? To whom is she connected?

SHEPHERD: She is sister to a gentleman who lived among us once – what was his name? Lived at Monkford – Mrs Croft's brother – bless me! what was his name? Anne, *you* will recall – ?

ANNE: Mr Wentworth.

SIR WALTER: Wentworth?

SIR WALTER *speaks the name – that of one of the great landed families of England – with deep respect.* ANNE *looks uncomfortable at this turn in the conversation.* LADY RUSSELL *continues to watch her discreetly.*

SHEPHERD: That's right! Wentworth, had the curacy of Monkford, some time back. You remember him, I'm sure.

SIR WALTER: Oh, Wentworth the *curate* – you misled me by the term 'gentleman', Shepherd. Mr Wentworth the curate was nobody; quite unconnected; nothing to do with the Strafford family. One does wonder how the names of so many of our nobility become so common. ANNE *suddenly stands and walks to the window, deeply agitated.*

SIR WALTER: Said I something amiss?

ELIZABETH (*quietly*): You remember, Father. The curate's
    brother. The sailor.
LADY RUSSELL: Let us not pursue it.
    SHEPHERD *and* MRS CLAY *look puzzled.* ANNE *returns
    to her seat.*
ANNE: Please excuse me . . . the fire . . . I became
    overheated, that is all.
    *This is an unlikely possibility in such a room, but nobody
    remarks on it. Adopting again his usual mode of behaviour
    towards* ANNE *— i.e., completely ignoring her existence —*
    SIR WALTER *comes to a decision.*
SIR WALTER: I am satisfied. (*To* SHEPHERD.) I empower
    you to proceed in the treaty. They may have possession
    at Michaelmas. And, Shepherd, with your consent, I
    wish to engage dear Mrs Clay to reside with us at Bath,
    as a companion for Elizabeth.
    He smiles engagingly at MRS CLAY, *who manages to
    blush.*
SHEPHERD: I can think of no higher privilege for my
    daughter, sir, than to accompany Miss Elliot in society.
LADY RUSSELL: What about Anne? Is Anne not companion
    enough for you?
ELIZABETH: Oh, Anne won't be coming, Lady Russell. I
    had a letter this morning from sister Mary, who is
    indisposed. She requires Anne's company at
    Uppercross, until her health improves; (*To* ANNE.) and
    since no one will want you in Bath, I am sure you had
    better stay here.
    ANNE *stares at the floor.* LADY RUSSELL *is livid.*

KELLYNCH – STAIRS. DAY.
Some days later. ANNE *is coming down the stairs with a sheaf
of papers in her hand, checking through lists as she walks. As*

*she nears the bottom, she hears approaching voices coming along
the hallway below.*

SIR WALTER: And thus we proceed to the dining-room,
  Admiral. The second-best silver will be at your
  disposal, Mrs Croft.
  SIR WALTER *leads* ADMIRAL *and* MRS CROFT *on a
  tour of the house, accompanied by* SHEPHERD. *Like a
  startled rabbit,* ANNE *stares at them over the banister.*

KELLYNCH – DINING-ROOM. NIGHT.
*A frosty last supper before the departure for Bath. Candles
flickering on the table. An atmosphere of stiff formality. Seated
are* SIR WALTER, ELIZABETH *and* ANNE, *waited on by a
large number of servants, many of whom are purely there for
decoration.* SIR WALTER's *table manners are exquisite.*

SIR WALTER: Instruct the staff to be civil to Admiral Croft,
  Anne, for I declare he is the best-looking sailor I have
  ever met.
  *A long silence punctuated only by the sound of cutlery on
  plates.*
SIR WALTER: Indeed, if my own man might be allowed the
  arranging of his hair, I should not be ashamed of being
  seen with him anywhere.
  ANNE *nods. Another long, dreary pause as they eat.*

KELLYNCH HALL. DAY.
The day of the ELLIOTS' *departure from Kellynch Hall. The
staff are formed up on the steps. The driveway is lined with
yeomen and peasants and their families, shivering in the wind,
in which blow showers of autumn leaves. A coach-and-four is
waiting. Behind it comes a more functional wagon, piled high
with luggage.* ANNE *waits at the top of the steps with the*

butlers. ELIZABETH *and* MRS CLAY *come out of the door, giggly and happy.*

ELIZABETH (*to* ANNE, *briskly*): I have not had time to speak to the gardener. Here is a list of the plants that are for Lady Russell. And this is a list of the books and music that I want sent on to Bath. Then you had better catalogue all the pictures, and clear your rubbish out of the store-room. And someone really ought to visit every house in the parish, as a take-leave. It is the Elliot way. ANNE *nods.* ELIZABETH *marches down the steps to the waiting carriage.* MRS CLAY *curtsies to* ANNE *and follows after.* SIR WALTER *comes out of the house in his fashionable travelling clothes. He turns to look back at the house, rather sadly.*

SIR WALTER (*quietly*): If only I'd had a son, all this would one day be his. – Be what use you can to your sister Mary, Anne.

ANNE: Yes, Father.

SIR WALTER: Lady Russell will bring you up to Bath after Christmas.

SIR WALTER *looks at* ANNE *for a moment, and gives a slight shake of his head, as if in disappointment at what he sees. Then he gets quickly into the carriage. The* COACHMAN *cracks his long whip and the carriage moves off down the drive. Before it is out of sight,* ANNE *slips back into the house.*

The tenants stare glumly after their departing landlord.

KELLYNCH HALL. DAY.
ANNE *walks through various of the day-rooms. In each, servants are engaged on throwing white dust-sheets over the furniture. The linen billows around* ANNE. *It's a sad picture, as if the deceased house is being wrapped in a shroud. On and on it*

10

goes: an ocean of white linen. More servants are busy on ladders, taking the family portraits off the walls.

KELLYNCH – STORE-ROOM. NIGHT.
By candlelight, ANNE *and a* MAID *work through the rubbish in the store-room. The* MAID *packs away old children's toys into trunks.* ANNE *sorts through a box of sheet music. She comes upon something that makes her catch her breath. It's her eight-year-old copy of the 'Navy List, 1806'. The sight unnerves her. As she picks up the volume, it falls open at a well-thumbed page. Inside, squashed flat, is a letter folded up into a paper boat: a memento.* ANNE *glances across at the* MAID, *who has noticed nothing, and quickly puts the volume away.*

KELLYNCH – DRAWING-ROOM. DAY.
ANNE *and* LADY RUSSELL *sit at a small table in the drawing-room, taking tea. The rest of the furniture is covered by dust-sheets. The fire is out.*

LADY RUSSELL: For eight years you have been too little from home, too little seen. And your spirits have never been high since your . . . disappointment. A larger society will improve them.
ANNE: But I so dislike Bath.
LADY RUSSELL: Only because you associate with it the passing of your dear mother.
ANNE: While my mother was alive there was moderation and economy in our home, and no need of moving out.
This is a statement with which LADY RUSSELL *cannot disagree. She gives a slight 'humph'. A pause.*
LADY RUSSELL: Do you travel directly to Uppercross?
ANNE: Yes. I prefer to be gone when his – when Admiral and Mrs Croft arrive. (*Quietly.*) I hope that they remember as little as my own people seem to do.

LADY RUSSELL: I have no desire to meet the new tenants of Kellynch Hall. I feel this break-up of your family exceedingly. Indeed, it angers me. I have done my best to stand in the place of your mother, and to offer the advice I believe she would have given. And now . . .

LADY RUSSELL *purses her lips and sucks in her breath.*

ANNE: Lady Russell . . . I have never said this . . .

LADY RUSSELL: Do not talk of it. We shall not talk of it.

ANNE (*forcing herself to do so, whilst staring at the floor*): I do not blame you; nor do I blame myself for having been guided by you. But I am now persuaded that in spite of the disapproval at home, and the anxiety attending his prospects, I should have been happier had I –

LADY RUSSELL: You were but nineteen, Anne! At nineteen, to involve yourself with a man who had nothing but himself to recommend him! Spirit and brilliancy, to be sure, but no fortune, and no connections! It was entirely prudent of you to reject him. (*Giving* ANNE *a book.*) Here are the new poems I told you of. Altogether, I care little for these 'romantics'. Do you?

KELLYNCH. DAY.

A dismal, grey day. ANNE *sits in a simple wagon, next to the* CARTER. *Her small trunk is behind them, next to a pig and a crate of geese. She takes a last look back at Kellynch Hall as the cart rattles down the driveway. Around them, great bonfires of fallen leaves are burning.*

UPPERCROSS. DAY.

The wagon drives into Uppercross village. They pass the Great House, an Elizabethan manor, with a multitude of high chimneys. The sight of it pleases ANNE. *They draw up outside* MARY's *house, a small farmhouse elevated into the young squire's residence. It could be very pretty, but in* MARY's *hands it's a shambles. As* ANNE *descends from the wagon, she glimpses* MARY's *face peeping out of the drawing-room window.* MARY *quickly ducks away.*

MARY'S HOUSE. DAY.
MARY *is lying feebly on the sofa in her small drawing-room as* ANNE *enters. A* MAID *helps* ANNE *off with her travelling clothes. In the hallway behind, the* CARTER *drags in her trunk.* ANNE *immediately begins to pick up the children's toys which are scattered around the floor, and put them in the toy basket. The furniture, once smart, has been battered by children, the walls have crayon on them, and there is a general untidiness around the house.*

MARY: So, you have come at last! I began to think I should never see you. I am so ill I can hardly speak. I haven't seen a creature the whole morning! Suppose I were to be seized in some dreadful way, and not able to ring the bell! – Lady Russell, I notice, would not come in person. I do not think she has been in this house three times this summer.

ANNE: Lady Russell cordially asked to be remembered to yourself and Charles.

MARY: Charles is out shooting. Haven't seen him since seven o'clock. He said he would not stay long; but he hasn't come back, has he? I do believe if Charles were to see me *dying*, he wouldn't believe there was anything the matter with me!

ANNE (*cheerfully*): Well, you know I always cure you when I come to Uppercross. How is everyone at the Great House?

13

MARY: I can give you no account of them. Not one of
them has been near me. It doesn't happen to suit the
Miss Musgroves, I suppose, to visit the sick.

ANNE: Perhaps you will see them before the morning is gone.

MARY: I don't want them, I assure you. My sisters-in-law
talk and laugh a great deal too much for one in my
condition. And Henrietta goes on and on about this
wretched curate from Winthrop whom she intends to
marry. Oh, Anne, why could you not have come earlier?
It is so unkind.

ANNE: My dear Mary, I really have had so much to do, I
could not have left Kellynch any sooner!

MARY: What can *you* possibly have had to do?

ANNE: A great many things, as a matter of fact.

MARY: Oh, well, dear me. – You haven't asked me one word
about our dinner at the Pooles' yesterday.

*MARY forgets herself, and gets up to trim a floral
arrangement at the other end of the room.*

ANNE: I thought you must have been obliged to give up the
engagement. . . ?

MARY swiftly recollects her illness, and lies down again.

MARY: Oh no, I was very well yesterday. But today I feel
like death.

ANNE (*smiles with resignation*): Had you a pleasant party?

MARY'S HOUSE. DAY.
The dining-room. MARY *has suddenly got over her indisposi-
tion, and finds herself able to attack a vast plate of cold meat –
ham, beef, tongue – and a jar of mustard.* ANNE *contents herself
with a delicate slice or two.*

MARY: Nothing remarkable. One always knows beforehand
what the dinner will be, and who will be there. And it is
so very uncomfortable, not having a carriage of one's

15

own. Charles's parents took me, and we were so crowded! They take up so much room! I was cramped into the back seat with Henrietta and Louisa, and I think it very likely that my illness today may be owing to it. – Do you know, Anne, I am feeling a little improved. Always assuming I do not relapse, shall we walk after luncheon to the Great House?

ANNE (*pleased*): I'd like that.

MARY: They ought to have called on you first, of course. They ought to have had the manners to know what is due to you as *my* sister.

GREAT HOUSE. DAY.
ANNE *and* MARY *walk through the park towards the Great House.*

ANNE: But I wouldn't dream of standing on ceremony with people I know so well as the Musgroves!

GREAT HOUSE. DAY.
The MUSGROVES' *drawing-room, decorated in the old style. A warm, cheery atmosphere, aided by roaring log fires in two huge old farmhouse grates. A sense of gaiety and good humour in this house which contrasts with Kellynch.* ANNE *and* MARY *stand in front of the seated* MRS MUSGROVE, *who's very fat and jolly. Her daughters,* LOUISA *and* HENRIETTA, *nineteen and twenty, manipulate a large harp into a prominent position in the room, which is already dominated by a brand-new pianoforte.*

MRS MUSGROVE: So Sir Walter and your sister are gone; and what part of Bath do you think they will settle in? *As* ANNE *opens her mouth to reply to this polite enquiry,* MRS MUSGROVE's *attention is caught by the harp.*

16

MRS MUSGROVE: *Must* that thing go exactly there, Henrietta?

HENRIETTA: Isn't it splendid, Mama?

LOUISA: It will sound very well with the pianoforte, don't you think, Anne?

ANNE *goes to the magnificent piano and plays a few chords.*

MRS MUSGROVE: What was wrong with my old spinet, I want to know, that it must make way for that great noisy article?

HENRIETTA: Oh, Anne, will you play, when next we give a dance? You play a great deal better than either of us, and we are wild for dancing.

MRS MUSGROVE: Oh yes, please, Miss Anne! Lord bless me! How those fingers of hers can fly about!

ANNE *smiles; she enjoys the rare compliment. The* MUSGROVES *laugh good-humouredly.*

MARY: I will play too if you wish. I am quite as accomplished as Anne.

MRS MUSGROVE (*graciously*): Why thank you, Mary.

LOUISA: But we all enjoy so much to watch you dancing, Mary. You are so light on your feet. And as you know, Anne does not care to dance.

They all look to ANNE.

ANNE (*with no bitterness*): No.

CHARLES MUSGROVE, MARY'*s husband, about the same age as* ANNE, *enters with his father,* MR MUSGROVE, *who is as fat as his wife. They are ruddy, hearty, jovial countryfolk. The men have been shooting. Their boots are caked in mud, but nobody cares. Some of their dogs — soaking wet — race in, shake themselves, and lie in front of the fire. The men greet* ANNE *very warmly; they're really pleased to see her. They bow cordially to* MRS MUSGROVE, MARY *and the girls.*

MR MUSGROVE: Miss Anne! What a great delight!

ANNE: Mr Musgrove, the delight is mine, to return once more to Uppercross.

MR MUSGROVE: You are most welcome here among us.

ANNE: You look well, Charles, very well.

CHARLES: Got a brace of pheasant this morning. And father hit a squab, but the dog couldn't find it. (*Laughter from the* MUSGROVES.) Feel pretty well, Anne, thank you, yes.

ANNE (*as quietly as she dares*): You were missed at luncheon, Charles.

CHARLES *sighs.*

MR MUSGROVE: Your father I trust is in health, Miss Anne?

MRS MUSGROVE: They've gone away to Bath, Papa, do you not remember me saying?

MR MUSGROVE: Ah yes, Bath, Bath.

LOUISA: I do hope *we* shall be at Bath this winter.

MR MUSGROVE (*with a smile*): Perhaps we may.

HENRIETTA: But remember, if we do go, we must be in a good situation.

LOUISA (*imploring*): Somewhere near the Circus, Papa, *please!*

MR MUSGROVE: Well, it's a big place, Bath.

MRS MUSGROVE: It's a great big place.

MR MUSGROVE: So I believe.

None of them have ever been there.

MARY (*anxiously*): Upon my word, I shall be well off, shan't I, when you are all gone away to be happy at Bath!

MRS MUSGROVE: Anne! Come and sit by the fire.

Cut to:

MRS MUSGROVE *speaks confidentially to* ANNE, *on the sofa, as general conversation continues elsewhere.*

MRS MUSGROVE: My dear, I make a rule of never interfering in my daughter-in-law's concerns; but I have to tell you that I have no very good opinion of the

19

way Mary curbs her children. Oh, they are fine healthy boys, but Lord bless me, how troublesome they can be!

Cut to:

MARY *speaks confidentially to* ANNE, *in another part of the room, as conversation continues elsewhere.*

MARY: Mrs Musgrove is forever advising me on the care of Little Charles and Walter, yet she gives them so many sweet things to eat that they invariably come home sick! Moreover, how am I supposed to keep them in order, when their father spoils them so much?

Cut to:

CHARLES *speaks confidentially to* ANNE.

CHARLES: I could manage the boys very well, were it not for Mary's interference. And I wish you could persuade her not to be always fancying herself ill.

Cut to:

ANNE's *back on the sofa, with* MRS MUSGROVE *once more bending her ear.* ANNE's *beginning to look a little giddy.*

MRS MUSGROVE: It is a very bad thing to be visited by children whom one can only keep in tolerable order by more cake than is good for them.

Cut to:

HENRIETTA *speaks confidentially to* ANNE.

HENRIETTA: Could you possibly, whilst you are here, give Mary a hint that it would be better if she were not so very tenacious about taking precedence over Mama? Nobody doubts her right to take precedence over Mama, but it is not becoming of her, always to insist on it.

Cut to:

LOUISA *speaks confidentially to* ANNE.

LOUISA: Mama doesn't care about etiquette. It's the cake she cares about.

Cut to:

MARY *speaks confidentially to* ANNE.

20

MARY: These people are apt to forget whose daughter I am!
– When you have a moment you must speak to Charles,
Anne, and persuade him I am very, very ill.
Cut to:
CHARLES *speaks confidentially to* ANNE.
CHARLES (*sighs deeply*): Oh, Anne . . .
ANNE *can only nod sympathetically to each of them. By
now she's looking quite exhausted. Something like this
always happens when she comes to Uppercross.*

GREAT HOUSE. DAY.
A little while later, HENRIETTA *is playing on the harp, with
everybody gathered round, smiling to each other, seemingly in
perfect harmony.* LOUISA, MARY *and* ANNE *stand together.*

LOUISA: And when will the Admiral take possession?
ANNE: At Michaelmas.
MARY: Let us hope they are not tardy about paying their
respects.
Everyone applauds as the recital ends.

MARY'S HOUSE. DAY.
MARY, ANNE *and* ADMIRAL *and* MRS CROFT *sit very
formally in* MARY'*s drawing-room, making polite, restrained
conversation.*

MARY: My husband is riding to hounds this morning,
Admiral, or he should have been here.
ADMIRAL: Naturally I am disappointed, Mrs Musgrove.
MARY: So too will he be; he has been curious to obtain a
close view of his father-in-law's tenant.
The ADMIRAL *smiles; this stuff doesn't bother him.* MRS
CROFT *turns to speak to* ANNE, *when the door crashes
open, and the boys,* CHARLES *and* WALTER, *come belting*

21

in. JEMIMA, *the nursery-maid, stands forlornly in the doorway. The* BOYS *run straight to the* ADMIRAL *and jump all over him.* MARY *is horrified.*

BOYS: Want to see the Admiral!

MARY: Charles! Walter!

ADMIRAL (*laughing*): No, no, let them be.

MRS CROFT: The Admiral loves children.

ADMIRAL: So, you want to sail on the high seas, do you, my lads? Well, you'll have to learn to go up and down with the swell, like this . . . !

In a second he has both BOYS *on his lap, being bumped up and down. They squeal with delight.* MARY *is embarrassed.* MRS CROFT *turns again to* ANNE.

MRS CROFT: It was you, and not your sister, I find, that my brother had the pleasure of being acquainted with, when he was in this country.

ANNE *has to look away, and breathe deeply. Suddenly her composure is gone. It appears to her that* MRS CROFT *is watching her closely.*

MRS CROFT: Perhaps you may not have heard that he is married . . . ?

ANNE: That is excellent news, Mrs Croft. I wish him every happiness.

MRS CROFT: With your permission I shall tell him so in my next letter.

ANNE: Please do.

MRS CROFT: Oh, and he has a new curacy, too, at last. They are settled in a parish in Shropshire.

ANNE *heaves a great inward sigh of relief.* MRS CROFT *looks over to where the* ADMIRAL *is playing with the excited* BOYS. *She smiles.* ANNE *studies her face closely, searching, perhaps, for a resemblance to the man she once knew.*

ADMIRAL: Now then, my lads – ever seen a boat made out of paper?

22

BOYS: No!

ADMIRAL: Watch very closely.

He takes a sheet of paper from the writing-desk, and begins to fold it into a paper boat. C.U. ANNE, who gives a deep inward sigh of recognition.

MRS CROFT (*to* MARY): I was telling Miss Anne of my brother Edward's good fortune in Shropshire. He is a curate.

MARY: A curate? How interesting.

ADMIRAL (*at work on his boat*): We are expecting soon another brother of my wife's. A seafaring brother, whom you will not know.

MARY: Oh, but we do know him, do we not, Anne? He visited these parts, when I was but a girl, and called at Kellynch Hall, some once or twice . . . ?

This with an enquiring look to ANNE which is entirely innocent.

ANNE: Yes.

MRS CROFT (*to* ANNE): I did not know you were acquainted with Frederick also.

ANNE: Yes. I believe you to have been in the Indies at that time.

ADMIRAL: There!

He has completed the paper boat. He holds it up. The BOYS are thrilled.

MARY'S GARDEN. DAY.

Next day. A stream runs through MARY's garden, not too far from the house. ANNE is playing with the BOYS by the stream. She crouches down to launch the paper boat into the water.

ANNE: There she goes! Hip hip –

BOYS: Hurrah!

ANNE: Hip hip –

BOYS: Hurrah!

The paper boat sails cheerfully down the stream, the BOYS *running alongside.* HENRIETTA *comes in through the garden gate.*

HENRIETTA: Good morning, Anne.

ANNE: Good morning.

HENRIETTA *is bubbling with excitement. She forgets her small-talk; she blurts out the news.*

HENRIETTA: Papa has met Captain Wentworth!

ANNE (*politely*): Indeed, has he?

HENRIETTA: Yes! Mama and he drove over to Kellynch, and *he* was there! He is just returned to England, or paid off, or something, and –

MARY *appears at the cottage window.*

MARY: Are you coming in, Henrietta? Or is my cottage insufficiently grand for you?

HENRIETTA: Oh, I may not stay, thank you, Mary. I am here solely to invite you to call at the Great House this evening –

ANNE: That is very kind.

HENRIETTA: – to meet Captain Frederick Wentworth. By every account a most charming and agreeable gentleman! And he is to call on us, tonight!

MARY: Oh! We shall be present, Henrietta, have no fear.

ANNE *is rigid with shock. She's going to meet again the man she once loved.*

ANNE'S BEDROOM. EVENING.

A spare little room under the eaves of the cottage, with a bed, a chest, some books, and a wash-stand. ANNE *puts on her bonnet, ready to go to the Great House. She glances at herself in the small mirror; she's dreading the visit. She hears cries from outside, and going to the window, sees a terrible sight.* JEMIMA *is running down the lane towards the house,*

24

shrieking. Behind her an old LABOURER *is doing his best to keep up, carrying the prone body of* LITTLE CHARLES *in his arms. Lastly comes* WALTER, *in floods of tears.* MARY *runs out of the house, screaming hysterically.* ANNE *quickly heads for the door.*

MARY'S HOUSE. NIGHT.
LITTLE CHARLES *has been laid on a sofa.* MARY *is weeping, comforted by* JEMIMA *and the* MAID. *The* APOTHECARY *speaks quietly to* ANNE.

APOTHECARY: I have reset the collar-bone.
ANNE: And the spine?
APOTHECARY: Time will tell.
ANNE: Should I put him to bed?
APOTHECARY: No, leave him where he is.
ANNE: What may I give him?
APOTHECARY: Water.
> CHARLES *dashes in, in his riding clothes. He's out of breath.*
CHARLES: What happened?
ANNE: Fell from a tree.
> CHARLES *drops to his knees by the boy's side.*

MARY'S HOUSE. NIGHT.
ANNE *kneels by the sleeping child, bathing his face with water.* CHARLES *is putting the final touches to his best evening-dress.* MARY *is furious with him. They speak in low voices.*

MARY: How can you contemplate such a thing? How can you abandon your son and heir – for a *dinner*?
CHARLES: The apothecary says he is going on well! He must rest, and be watched. What more is there for me to do? I

25

do so want to meet this Captain Wentworth. – Where are my gloves? The white ones?

CHARLES *leaves the room and goes upstairs.* MARY *slumps disconsolately.*

ANNE: Nursing does not belong to a man, Mary. It is not his province.

MARY: I am as fond of my child as any mother; but I have not the nerves for the sickroom. This is always my luck. If there is anything disagreeable going on, men are sure to get out of it.

ANNE: But could you be comfortable, spending the whole evening away from Little Charles?

MARY: If his father can, why shouldn't I?

ANNE: Then go along and dine at the Great House. Leave the boy to my care.

MARY: Dear me! That's a very good thought! You don't mind?

ANNE *shakes her head.* MARY *immediately starts to put on her bonnet.*

MARY: I too wish to meet Captain Wentworth. And you, Anne, are by far the properest person to sit with the boy, for you haven't a mother's feelings, have you? After all, it only harasses me.

GREAT HOUSE. NIGHT.
We view the dining-room of the Great House from outside. Each of the splendid high windows is ablaze with light. The company within are having a marvellous time: there is animated conversation and laughter. We see only the back of WENTWORTH's *head; ranged before him are the faces of* MRS MUSGROVE, HENRIETTA, LOUISA *and* MARY, *all glowing with adulation and barely-contained sexual hysteria.*

26

MARY'S HOUSE. NIGHT.

One oil-lamp burns, in stark contrast to the merriment of the previous scene. ANNE *sits by the sofa with the sleeping child. We can hear the wind in the trees. Otherwise silence.*

ANNE *mops the child's sweating brow.*

MARY'S HOUSE. DAY.

ANNE *and* MARY *are eating breakfast the following morning.* LITTLE CHARLES *remains on the sofa.*

MARY: He did enquire after you. Slightly. As might suit a former slight acquaintance. He was very attentive to me, however, and Charles and he made instant friends. In fact I believe they are to shoot together this morning.

ANNE: But he will not call here?

MARY: No. On account of the child.

ANNE (*just a hint of sarcasm*): Oh. The child.

She is beginning to think WENTWORTH *is avoiding her. Just then* CHARLES *appears at the window, breathless.*

CHARLES: We are just setting off! I am come for my dogs! Captain Wentworth follows, with my sisters – may he wait on you, Mary?

MARY (*wiping crumbs from her mouth*): Why certainly –

CHARLES: Here he comes now!

CHARLES *goes. There is a knock at the front door.* MARY *hastily composes herself, and rises to meet the guests.* ANNE *sits open-mouthed in terror and surprise, as if struck by lightning. Their door is opened by the* MAID. MARY *gives* ANNE *a poke in the arm.* ANNE *rises as* LOUISA *and* HENRIETTA *come in, followed by* WENTWORTH, *in uniform. He is indeed a good-looking man, but with a melancholy side, a deep pool somewhere.*

27

MAID: The Miss Musgroves, ma'am, and Captain Wentworth.

The women all curtsy, lightly.

MARY: It is most pleasant to see you again so soon, Captain.

WENTWORTH: Mrs Musgrove. How is your boy?

MARY: Much better, thank you; he has taken some broth. – I believe, Captain, that you are acquainted with my older sister Anne?

WENTWORTH (*politely*): We did meet once.

ANNE: Captain Wentworth.

For the briefest moment they look directly at each other. His gaze is neutral: it's impossible to tell what he's thinking. ANNE *holds his stare. But behind her, her fingers curl tightly around the back of her chair.*

WENTWORTH: I hope Little Charles makes a speedy recovery, Mrs Musgrove. Henrietta and Louisa swear he's quite a character, when fit.

The girls giggle, and WENTWORTH *smiles. But* ANNE *barely hears this conversation. The room seems to close in around her, and the sound to become a babble of words. Outwardly, she remains composed; but inside, she's spinning.*

WENTWORTH: Your husband, I hear, is a very decent shot. Better not let him grab the best position. And I see I have intruded on your breakfast. Forgive me. – Good day.

WENTWORTH *bows to the ladies, and turns to leave.*

HENRIETTA: Louisa, shall we walk with them?

LOUISA: Oh yes!

MARY: Oh! Then so shall I.

MARY *grabs her shawl. They all file out, and are gone in a second.* ANNE *holds on to the back of the chair, breathing deeply.*

COPSE. DAY.

CHARLES and WENTWORTH are positioned some distance from a copse, on the side of a hill. A little way off stand MARY, LOUISA and HENRIETTA, watching the shoot. Through the copse come the beaters, making a terrific noise. Some birds go up, and the sportsmen aim and fire. They each bring down a bird. The ladies applaud excitedly. WENTWORTH turns to CHARLES, puzzled.

WENTWORTH: Do your women often come shooting?
CHARLES (smirking): Not that often, Frederick, no.

MARY'S HOUSE. DAY.
ANNE is sitting with LITTLE CHARLES when MARY returns.

ANNE (mischievously): Had you good hunting, Mary?
MARY: Upon my word yes, we bagged, oh, ever so many birds. But that Captain Wentworth is not very gallant towards you, Anne. When Henrietta asked him what he thought of you, he said you were so altered he would not have known you again.

ANNE'S BEDROOM. DAY.
ANNE stands in front of the mirror on the wash-stand, staring intently at her face. She comes to the reluctant conclusion that she must agree with WENTWORTH's judgement. She unpins and lets down her hair, but it doesn't help much. She still looks prematurely middle-aged. She pinches her sallow cheek, and grimaces at her appearance.

GREAT HOUSE. NIGHT.
WENTWORTH has become a regular visitor to Uppercross. He seems very relaxed at the dinner party which is now in progress.

30

He looks extremely manly and attractive. In eight years, it would seem his *appearance has improved. Present around the table are* MR *and* MRS MUSGROVE, HENRIETTA, LOUISA, CHARLES, MARY, ANNE, WENTWORTH, ADMIRAL CROFT, MRS CROFT. *They are eating a syllabub dessert.* WENTWORTH *and* ANNE *do not look at each other if they can possibly avoid it. Otherwise it is a merry affair.*

WENTWORTH: You suppose sailors live on board without anything to eat? Or any cooks? Or any servants? Or any knife and fork to use? We ain't savages, Louisa! (*Laughter.*) Let me tell you about my first command. The *Asp.* I sailed away in the *Asp* in the year eighteen-six.

HENRIETTA: We have a Navy List. We shall look her up!

MR MUSGROVE: They made me send for it from Plymouth, Captain.

LOUISA *fetches it from a sideboard. The girls open it up on the table.*

WENTWORTH: You won't find her in a new List, I'm afraid. She's been broken up for scrap. I was the last man to command her, eight years ago, and she was hardly fit for service then. Nearly sank on several occasions, the *Asp* . . . and then I should only have been a gallant Captain Wentworth, in a small paragraph at the bottom corner of the newspaper . . . and you would never have heard of me.

LOUISA (*horrified*): Yet still you took her out?

MARY: Oh, my word!

WENTWORTH: The Admiralty like to entertain themselves now and then with sending a few hundred men to sea in a ship not fit to be employed. But among the thousands that may just as well go to the bottom as not, it is impossible for them to distinguish the ones who will least be missed.

CHARLES (*amidst laughter*): Well said!

ADMIRAL: Never was a better sloop than the *Asp* in her day. Lucky fellow to get her! Lucky fellow to get anything so soon!

WENTWORTH: I felt my luck, I assure you. I was well satisfied with my appointment. I was extremely keen, at the time – in the year six – to be at sea. Most extremely keen. I badly wanted to be doing something.

These words cause ANNE *pain, but she cannot acknowledge it.*

ADMIRAL: Naturally you did. What should a young fellow like you do ashore, for half a year together? If a man has no wife, he wants to be afloat again.

WENTWORTH: Well, I had no wife. In the year six.

He cannot refrain from the briefest glance towards ANNE, *who avoids his eyes.*

LOUISA: Then, Captain Wentworth, what came next?

WENTWORTH: The *Laconia*.

LOUISA: The *Laconia*! Find the *Laconia*!

The girls pore over the Navy List.

WENTWORTH: Ah, those were great days, when I had the *Laconia* . . . !

HENRIETTA: Here she is! HMS *Laconia*: seventy-four gun frigate, second class!

WENTWORTH: A friend and I had a fine cruise off the West Indies in the *Laconia*, taking enough privateers to be very entertaining, and make us quite rich. You remember Captain Harville, Admiral? An excellent fellow! I wonder what's become of him?

ADMIRAL: Did not you bring Mrs Harville and her three children round from Portsmouth to Plymouth, that spring?

WENTWORTH: So? What of it?

ADMIRAL (*triumphantly*): Ha!

WENTWORTH: I'd bring anything of Harville's from the world's end, if he wanted me to.

ADMIRAL: This is a man famous in the Navy for declaring he will never have a woman on his ship!

MRS MUSGROVE: What, never?

MRS CROFT: Except for a ball, of course!

Laughter. WENTWORTH *is unsettled.*

WENTWORTH: It's from no lack of gallantry towards women, Mrs Musgrove. Rather the reverse. You see, it's impossible to make the accommodation on board ship suitable for a party of ladies.

MRS CROFT: Oh, Frederick! Why, I have lived on five!

WENTWORTH: But you were living with your husband – yes – and you were the only woman on board.

MRS CROFT: That is not to the purpose. I hate to hear you talking as if all women were fine ladies, instead of rational creatures. We none of us expect to be in smooth water all our days.

ADMIRAL: When he has got a wife, Sophia, he will sing a different tune. When he is married, if we have the good luck to live to another war, we shall see him very thankful to anybody that will bring him his wife.

There is laughter from the others, and embarrassed grins from the MUSGROVE GIRLS. ANNE *watches it all, detached.* WENTWORTH's *pride is hurt.*

WENTWORTH: Huh! Why – when – when married people start to attack me, I – (*Lost for words, he rises, and bows.*) Mrs Musgrove.

WENTWORTH *leaves the room, but not in such a way as to cause offence. The girls smile behind their hands. A brief silence.* MRS MUSGROVE *immediately goes into hostess mode.*

MRS MUSGROVE: What a great traveller you must have been, ma'am.

33

MRS CROFT: I have crossed the Atlantic four times, and have been once to the East Indies, and in different places about home: Cork, and Lisbon, and Gibraltar. But I never was in the West Indies – we do not call Bermuda or Bahama the West Indies, Mrs Musgrove, as you know.

CHARLES: I do not think mama has ever called them anything in the whole course of her life, Mrs Croft. *More laughter.* ANNE *is very impressed with* MRS CROFT: *she would like to be as confident as her. Now* WENTWORTH *has gone she feels able to speak.*

ANNE: But did you never suffer any sickness, Mrs Croft?

MRS CROFT: No. The only time that I ever fancied myself unwell, or had any ideas of danger, was the winter that I passed by myself at Deal, when the Admiral – Captain Croft then – was away in the North Seas. That I did not like. But as long as we could be together, nothing ever ailed me, not a thing.

The ADMIRAL *smiles tenderly at her.*

GREAT HOUSE. NIGHT.
Later that evening. In the drawing-room the furniture has been cleared for dancing. ANNE *plays the piano, happy to be able to keep her head down over the keys as the others dance a country jig: the couples are* ADMIRAL *and* MRS CROFT, WENTWORTH *and* LOUISA, MR MUSGROVE *and* HENRIETTA, CHARLES *and* MARY. *The enormous* MRS MUSGROVE *sits it out.*

ANNE *looks up to see* WENTWORTH *staring at her, coolly, as he dances: 'observing her altered features, perhaps, trying to trace in them the ruins of the face which had once charmed him.' Hastily she turns back to her music. But as* WENTWORTH *and* LOUISA *next sweep by her in the course of the dance, she hears* LOUISA *saying:*

LOUISA: Oh, no, never. She has quite given up dancing.

    Then they are gone. Shortly the music comes to an end and the dancers rest. ANNE *wanders to an open window for a breath of air. When she returns to the piano,* WENT-WORTH *is sitting on the stool, trying to pick out a naval air with one finger for the benefit of the* MISS MUSGROVES *and* MARY, *who are gathered round. He skips up as he sees* ANNE *approaching.*

WENTWORTH: I beg your pardon, madam, this is your seat.

ANNE (*flustered*): Not at all, I –

    But he goes, and the women trail after him.

UPPERCROSS. NIGHT.

HENRY HAYTER *approaches the Great House on a rather scraggy-looking pony. He dismounts cheerfully, hearing the sounds of music and laughter within.*

GREAT HOUSE. NIGHT.

A further dance is in progress in the drawing-room, more lively than the first. This time WENTWORTH *dances with* HENRIETTA. *A* SERVANT *opens the door to admit* HENRY HAYTER. *The curate's clothes are a little shabby. He enters just as* WENTWORTH *is twirling* HENRIETTA *around in the middle of the floor, both of them laughing delightedly, flirtatiously.* ANNE *looks up from the piano, sees* HAYTER, *and stops playing. Everyone turns to look at the new arrival – except* HENRIETTA, *who can't take her eyes off* WENTWORTH. HAYTER's *good humour turns instantly to jealousy.*

CHARLES: Henry!

    A nasty pause. LOUISA *feels someone ought to make the introductions.*

LOUISA: Captain Wentworth, this is our cousin from Winthrop, Henry Hayter.

WENTWORTH *nods cordially at* HAYTER, *unaware of any problem.* HAYTER, *mortified at what he's seen, turns straight round and walks out again.* HENRIETTA *turns to the puzzled* WENTWORTH *and shrugs 'no idea what's wrong with him'.*

MARY'S HOUSE. DAY.
Luncheon in the dining-room. MARY, CHARLES *and* ANNE *eat soup.*

CHARLES: Twenty thousand pounds! He told me! He's made twenty thousand pounds in the war! It would be a capital match for either of my sisters. – Which do you think most probable, Anne, to marry the Captain? Mary gives it for Henrietta. I am for Louisa.

ANNE *contents herself with floating a little piece of bread in her soup, and pushing it around with her spoon. She doesn't eat. The others slurp away.*

MARY: I do not think Henrietta has the right to throw herself away on Henry Hayter. She must think of her family. It is very inconvenient of any young woman to give bad connections to those who have not been used to them.

CHARLES: Henry is a good-natured, good sort of a fellow, and stands to inherit very pretty property, at Winthrop; Henrietta might do far worse. If she has him, and Louisa can get Captain Wentworth, I shall be well satisfied. What say you, Anne? Which one is the Captain in love with?

ANNE *manages a smile.*

36

GREAT HOUSE WOODS. DAY.

ANNE *walks alone through the Great House woods. The house itself is just visible in the distance. A chill wind blows the leaves down in showers from the trees.* ANNE *shuffles through great piles of yellow leaves on the path. Everywhere she looks, things seem to be drooping and dying. She hears voices as she nears a glade. Sitting on an ornate bench are* HENRIETTA *and* LOUISA, *deep in conversation. As they come into* ANNE's *sight,* LOUISA *is talking animatedly, and* HENRIETTA *is sitting silently and staring at the ground. We can't quite hear what is said.* ANNE *judges it best to turn around and walk away. The girls do not notice her.*

MARY'S HOUSE. DAY.

ANNE *and* MARY *in the drawing-room.* LITTLE CHARLES *is sitting up at the table with his arm in a sling. The three of them are attempting a jigsaw puzzle. Through the window* MARY *sees* HENRIETTA *and* LOUISA *passing down the lane. They look serious.* MARY *races to the window.*

MARY: Good morning! Will you come in and sit with us a little?

LOUISA: Thank you, but we are to go a long walk, Mary.

MARY: I am fond of a long walk.

LOUISA: This is a very long walk.

MARY: Why is every body always supposing I am not a good walker? I should like to join you very much. Come, Anne, let us put on our wraps.
The looks on the girls' faces tell ANNE *that they would rather go alone.*

ANNE: Mary, we have our puzzle to finish –
But MARY *is already heading for the door.*

37

UPPERCROSS. DAY.

As HENRIETTA, LOUISA, ANNE *and* MARY *leave the village, they meet* CHARLES *and* WENTWORTH *returning from shooting. 'Good mornings' are said all round.*

MARY (*to* WENTWORTH): We are going on a long walk.
WENTWORTH: You tired, Charles? I'm not. Shall we join the ladies on their walk?
  So the men give their guns to their VALET *and fall in with the women.* HENRIETTA *and* LOUISA *lead the way – they are clearly in charge of the route.*

FIELDS. DAY.

A pale, wintry sun is shining: one of the last fine days of the year. The party follows a narrow path across a field. They make a gradual ascent. A short way off a number of labourers are ploughing with shire-horses. LOUISA *has attached herself to* WENTWORTH; HENRIETTA *walks with* CHARLES *and* MARY. *They come to a stile, and, as she waits to climb it,* ANNE *overhears this conversation:*

WENTWORTH (*on the stile*): I wonder where the gig will overturn today?
LOUISA (*trying not to laugh*): Oh, do not be cruel.
WENTWORTH: But it happens every time they go out! He's a first-rate sailor, but on land . . . Fortunately my sister is as happy to be tossed into the ditch as not.
  He jumps down. LOUISA *climbs the stile.*
LOUISA: Well, if I loved a man, as she loves the Admiral, I should do just the same; nothing would ever separate us, and I would rather be overturned by him, than driven safely by somebody else.
WENTWORTH (*warmly*): Fine words, Louisa.

38

WENTWORTH *is preparing to hand her down from the stile, when she suddenly jumps. With a laugh, he catches her, and sets her safely on the ground.* ANNE, *following behind, has to make her own way over the stile.*

HILL. DAY.
The party gains the summit of the highest hill, and begins to descend the far side. Way beneath them a group of farm buildings comes into view.

MARY: Bless my soul! That's Winthrop.
CHARLES: I see Henry's finished the new barn.
> HENRIETTA *blushes. Winthrop is the last place* MARY *wants to go — or wants* HENRIETTA *to go.*
MARY: Well, now I think we had better turn back; I am feeling excessively tired. Come along, Henrietta.
> HENRIETTA *turns, ready to do as* MARY *wants. But* LOUISA *stops her, forcefully.* CHARLES *has finally got the picture.*
CHARLES: Now we are come this far, I did ought to call on my Aunt Hayter. Mary, will you accompany me?
MARY: Certainly not.
CHARLES: You might rest a quarter of an hour in her kitchen.
MARY: Oh, no, indeed! Walking back up this hill will do me more harm than any sitting down in her kitchen will do me good. I intend to rest here, thank you, and then go home. Henrietta may rest with me. She does not want to go down there either. Do you, dear?
> HENRIETTA *bites her lip.*
CHARLES (*crossly*): Well, I shall do my duty to my aunt.
> CHARLES *sets off.* LOUISA *grabs* HENRIETTA*'s arm and pulls her along after* CHARLES. MARY *sighs and sits down on a fallen tree.*

39

MARY (*to* WENTWORTH): It is very unpleasant, having such connections! But I assure you, I have never been in that house above twice in my life.

ANNE sees WENTWORTH *give* MARY *an artificial smile, and turn away with a contemptuous look. He searches for* LOUISA. *She is now coming back up the path towards them, leaving* CHARLES *and* HENRIETTA *to go down alone. She skips up to* WENTWORTH.

LOUISA: Shall we try to glean some nuts from the hedgerow?

ANNE sits with MARY. WENTWORTH *and* LOUISA *go through an opening and disappear from sight along the far side of a hedgerow. It irritates* MARY *that they have gone.*

MARY: My seat is damp. I am sure Louisa has found a better.

ANNE: Leave her be, Mary.

MARY: No, I will not be damp.

MARY gets up and wanders after LOUISA. ANNE *stays where she is, enjoying the view. In a moment she hears* WENTWORTH *and* LOUISA *coming back towards her; they cannot see her.* ANNE *keeps very still and listens as they approach.*

LOUISA: I could not bear such nonsense. I would not be turned back from a thing I had determined to do, by the airs and interference of such a person! I am not so easily persuaded.

WENTWORTH: Would she have turned back, then, but for you?

LOUISA: I am ashamed to say that she would.

WENTWORTH: Henrietta's lucky to have you for a sister. Stick always to your purpose, Louisa. Be firm; I will like you the more for it.

A brief pause. We watch ANNE. *She can hardly breathe.*
40

LOUISA (*moving on*): Mary has a great deal too much of the
    Elliot pride. We all wish that Charles had married Anne
    instead.
WENTWORTH: Did he want to marry Anne?
LOUISA: Did you not know?
WENTWORTH: . . . Do you mean she refused him?
LOUISA: Yes.
WENTWORTH: When was that?
LOUISA: About a year before he married Mary. If only Anne
    had accepted him. . . ! We should all have liked *her* a
    great deal better. My parents think that it was Lady
    Russell's doing; that my brother being not philosophical
    enough for her taste, she persuaded Anne to refuse
    him.
    And they are gone along the hedgerow. ANNE *sits as if*
    frozen to the ground; internally she is extremely agitated.
    MARY *approaches, grumpily, having failed to find*
    LOUISA.
MARY: I had better have your seat, Anne, if you have had
    your rest.

HILL. DAY.
A little later. CHARLES *and* HENRIETTA *come up the hill*
bringing a sheepish but happy HAYTER *with them. He and*
HENRIETTA *hold hands, discreetly.*

LANE. DAY.
The party walks along a lane, heading back to Uppercross,
without HAYTER. ANNE *is tired.* WENTWORTH *notices this.*
CHARLES *and* MARY *keep as much distance between them as*
possible; he amuses himself by scything the heads off wild flowers
with a stick. A gig drives towards them, containing ADMIRAL
and MRS CROFT.

WENTWORTH: Good day, sir! We have been to Winthrop
and back!

MRS CROFT: The ladies must be exhausted.

ADMIRAL: We can offer a seat for one; it will save full a mile.
All the women politely decline. WENTWORTH *skips up to
have a quiet word with his sister.* MRS CROFT *then looks
at* ANNE.

MRS CROFT: Anne, I am sure *you* are tired. Do let us have
the pleasure of taking you home.

ANNE (*tired, but unwilling*): But there is no room.

ADMIRAL: Nonsense! Sophy and I will squash up! Were we
all as slim as you, we'd seat four!
*ANNE is standing by the gig. Before she quite knows what
is happening,* WENTWORTH, *standing behind her, has his
hands on her waist, his face at her shoulder. He says one
word.*

WENTWORTH (*quietly*): Please.
ANNE experiences a maelstrom of sensations as WENT-
WORTH *lifts her briskly and courteously up and into the
gig. She has felt his touch, smelt his smell . . . In an instant
she is seated, and the* ADMIRAL *cracks the reins. The
others call 'goodbye' as the gig rattles off.* ANNE *turns and
catches* WENTWORTH's *eye. He hastily looks away.*
Close shot of ANNE, *inwardly reeling.*

LANE. DAY.
The ADMIRAL *drives recklessly into Uppercross.* MRS CROFT
and ANNE *cling on to whatever they can find.*

ADMIRAL: I wish Frederick would spread a little more
canvas, and bring us home one of those nice young
ladies to Kellynch. This hesitation comes of the peace;
if it were war, he would have settled it long ago. Do you

not think, Sophy, that your brother is ready to fall in love?

MRS CROFT: I think my brother is ready to make a foolish match, George. Anybody between fifteen and thirty may have him for the asking. A little beauty, a few smiles, and a few compliments to the Navy, and he is a lost man.

MRS CROFT *catches* ANNE *staring at her open-mouthed, and grins at her.*

GREAT HOUSE. DAY.
WENTWORTH, CHARLES, MARY, HENRIETTA *and* LOUISA, *their boots muddy from the walk, are recovering in front of a blazing fire.* ANNE, *who arrived back first, is dispensing steaming mugs of hot chocolate.* WENTWORTH *reads a letter.*

CHARLES: Is it a love letter, Frederick?

WENTWORTH (*laughs*): No, it's from my old friend Harville. He's settled in Lyme! – how far away is that?

CHARLES: I should say about sixteen, seventeen miles.

WENTWORTH: Then I'll ride there tomorrow!

LOUISA *looks glum.*

CHARLES: You are fond of this Harville, I think.

WENTWORTH: I am. We had great sport together, in far corners of the world. He's not in good health – a leg wound, got in the war. But if you could meet him, Charles, I'm sure you'd love him as I do.

CHARLES: Well, why don't we make a visit, all together? I've long had a wish to see Lyme.

LOUISA: Oh, so have I, Charles, oh, let us go, *please*!

HENRIETTA: May we take Anne, too?

CHARLES: Let it be Anne's treat. Soon she must leave us for Bath.

43

LOUISA: We're going to Lyme, Mary!
MARY: I do not like the sea.

SEASHORE. DAY.
Lyme Regis. ANNE, HENRIETTA, LOUISA, MARY,
CHARLES *and* WENTWORTH *stand at the water's edge,
gazing at the splendour of the sea.* WENTWORTH *breathes
deeply of the salt air.* CHARLES *can't resist skimming a few
stones.* MARY *gives the ocean a bit of a sideways look, as if it
were some strange, unpredictable beast.*

LYME. DAY.
*The party walks towards the harbour. A number of small boats
are bobbing at their moorings.*

WENTWORTH: Before we enter Harville's house, I must
warn you that lodging there is a Captain Benwick, who
was my first lieutenant on the *Laconia*. He was devoted
to Harville's sister, and was set to marry her on our
return.

HARVILLE'S HOUSE. DAY.
The party approaches HARVILLE'*s house, a rickety little
weatherboard cottage on the quayside. It has small, mullioned,
bay windows and doors at odd angles. A telescope can be seen in
the front room.*

WENTWORTH: But Phoebe died whilst we were still at sea.

HARVILLE'S HOUSE. DAY.
Crammed into HARVILLE'*s front room are all of the
Uppercross party plus* HARVILLE, MRS HARVILLE, BEN-
WICK, *and the three* HARVILLE CHILDREN. *The room is*

small and low. It's hung about with fishing nets, and strewn
with totems of carved wood, exotic mementoes of foreign lands,
and nautical paraphernalia. MARY *looks about her in silent*
horror. The HARVILLE CHILDREN *are very sweet and well-*
behaved, though poor.

   WENTWORTH, HARVILLE *and* BENWICK *have their arms*
around each other like a rugby scrum, and are roaring with
laughter and slapping each other on the back. The Uppercross
women watch with great curiosity: they've never seen men
behave like this before. CHARLES *admires it hugely.*

WENTWORTH: Damn my eyes, it does me good to see you!
HARVILLE: Any friends of yours are welcome in my house.
   WENTWORTH *attempts to adopt a pose of formality and*
   correctness.
WENTWORTH: Ladies, Charles, may I introduce – (*He*
   collapses with laughter before he can finish.) – Captain
   Harville –
   HARVILLE, *supporting himself with a stick, bows low to*
   the ladies.
WENTWORTH: – and Captain Benwick.
   BENWICK *also bows, but he looks suddenly sad and*
   forlorn. ANNE *catches his eye momentarily.* MRS
   HARVILLE *turns to the visitors, with a kindly smile.*
MRS HARVILLE: I'm very happy to meet you all. You've
   certainly cheered us up. Please, treat our home as if it
   were your own.
HARVILLE: You must stay to supper! (*To his wife.*) Have we
   food?
   MARY'*s eyes widen in amazement.*
WENTWORTH: Remember what we ate in Menorca?
BENWICK: Octopus!
   The sailors roar with laughter at the memory. The
   Uppercross women can't believe what they're hearing.

THE COBB. DAY.

The whole party, except MRS HARVILLE *and children, walk out to the end of the Cobb. The three Navy men go first, laughing and talking. Some way behind,* ANNE *walks with* LOUISA *and* MARY. HENRIETTA *and* CHARLES *follow.*

LOUISA: Oh, I do admire the Navy. These sailors have more worth than any other set of men in England.
Close on ANNE : *she heartily assents, and inwardly dies, thinking to herself, 'These would have been my friends, if . . .'*

THE COBB. DAY.

ANNE *and* BENWICK *are at the very end of the Cobb, staring out at the rough sea. The rest of the party are a little way off.*

ANNE: And what do you find to occupy yourself with in Lyme, Captain Benwick?
BENWICK: I read.
ANNE (*with an engaging smile*): Well, what do you read, Captain Benwick?
BENWICK: Poetry.
ANNE: We are living through a great age for poetry, I think.
BENWICK (*surprised*): You read it too, Miss Elliot? Do you prefer 'Marmion' or 'The Lady of the Lake'?
ANNE: 'Like the dew on the mountain,
      Like the foam on the river – '
BENWICK: 'Like the bubble on the fountain,
      Thou art gone, and for ever.'
They exchange a moment of pleasure in finding a shared interest.

INN. NIGHT.
After supper. The Uppercross party, joined by HARVILLE *and*
BENWICK, *occupies the inn's saloon.* HARVILLE *smokes a*
pipe. ANNE *is sitting in a corner next to* BENWICK. *They are*
separated slightly from the main group, whose conversation goes
on around them.

BENWICK: 'Fare thee well! thus disunited,
    Torn from every nearer tie,
    Sear'd in heart, and lone, and blighted,
    More than this I scarce can die.'
ANNE (*a little shocked*): I do not know that one.
BENWICK: Byron.
ANNE: . . . You ought perhaps to include a larger allowance
    of prose in your daily study. Too much poetry may be
    . . . unsafe.
BENWICK: Thank you for your kindness. But you cannot
    know the depth of my despair. Phoebe would have
    married me before I went to sea. But I told her . . . (*He*
    chokes back tears.) I told her we must wait. For money.
    (*Bitterly.*) Money!
ANNE: Come now, Captain Benwick, come now. You will
    rally again. You must. Why, you are younger than I am.
BENWICK: You have no conception of what I have lost.
ANNE: Yes, I have.
    From across the room, WENTWORTH *is watching them*
    intently.

THE COBB. DAY.
Early next morning. ANNE *and* HENRIETTA *walk on the*
Cobb. ANNE *looks better than she has done for a long time.*
They are rather surprised to see LOUISA *and* WENTWORTH
walking along the sea wall towards them. They say their 'good
mornings'.

LOUISA: (*embarrassed*): We are just on our way back for breakfast.

HENRIETTA: We too.

They go along a strip of shingle beach, and come to the steps leading up to the road. A gentleman of about thirty (MR ELLIOT) is preparing to come down. He is wealthy and urbane. He's a widower, wearing a black band on his hat. He stops to give way, and bows. They ascend and pass him. ANNE's face catches his eye. He looks at her with admiration. The sea air has improved her complexion considerably. WENTWORTH notices the man's attention to her, and ANNE notices WENTWORTH; he gives her a bright, momentary glance, as if he suddenly saw the old Anne Elliot again. ANNE experiences a delicious feeling: rediscovering something she thought forever lost.

INN. DAY.

In her room at the inn, ANNE takes off her bonnet and walking cape in front of the mirror, and prepares to dress for breakfast. She is pleased with the colour in her cheeks. She considers rearranging her hair. She grins at her reflection, pleased that WENTWORTH was jealous of the other man.

INN CORRIDOR. DAY.

ANNE leaves her room and makes her way along the corridor. MR ELLIOT comes out of an adjoining room and almost collides with her.

ELLIOT: Madam, I do apologise.

ANNE: It is nothing, sir.

He bows and stands aside to let her pass, but there is no mistaking the way he looks at her: he finds her attractive. She glows.

49

INN DINING-ROOM. DAY.

At breakfast are MARY, CHARLES, WENTWORTH, LOUISA
and HENRIETTA. *The* LANDLORD *and a* MAID *serve them.*
They drink chocolate, and are eating something they find
unusual, which causes great mirth. A light-hearted holiday
atmosphere. ANNE *comes in to join them.*

CHARLES (*to* ANNE): Look – kippers for breakfast!
    WENTWORTH *smiles at* LOUISA, *who is tucking in with*
    gusto. MARY *pushes her plate away in disgust.*
MARY (*to* LANDLORD): Fetch me a piece of dry toast, and
    some jam.
    Everybody laughs good-naturedly at her. The LAND-
    LORD *sends the* MAID *out for the toast.* CHARLES *looks*
    out of the window (a bay window on the first floor).
CHARLES: Whose curricle is that, Landlord? It looks pretty
    fine.
LANDLORD: A gentleman of means, sir – come in last night
    from Sidmouth, on his way to Bath. A Mr Elliot.
MARY: Elliot? Mr Elliot?
    They all rush to the window. WENTWORTH *follows at a*
    more leisurely pace. They are just in time to see MR
    ELLIOT *leave the front door of the inn, climb into his*
    coach, and be driven away. There is a glimpse of a coat of
    arms on the door of the coach.
WENTWORTH (*with half a glance at* ANNE): It's the man we
    passed on the beach.
MARY (*craning to look*): Bless me! It must be our cousin! (*To*
    LANDLORD.) Did his servant say if he belonged to the
    Kellynch family?
LANDLORD: No, ma'am; though he do say his master'll be a
    Baronet one day.
MARY: There! It's him! Mr Elliot! The heir to Kellynch
    Hall! Do you think he had the Elliot countenance? – I
    hardly looked at him, I was looking at the horses, but I

think he had something of the Elliot countenance, do not you, Anne? How very extraordinary! What a pity we'd no chance to introduce ourselves!

ANNE (*quietly*): Mary, recall that father and Mr Elliot have not been on speaking terms for some years. They would neither of them wish us to introduce ourselves.

WENTWORTH (*looking straight at* ANNE): Quite lucky, then, that you didn't bump into him.

THE COBB. DAY.
LOUISA, WENTWORTH, HENRIETTA, CHARLES *and* MARY *walk along the top of the high sea-wall of the Cobb.* ANNE *and* BENWICK *walk below, shielded from the wind. They smile shyly at each other.*

BENWICK: I have enjoyed our debates.

ANNE (*smiles*): I too.

BENWICK: I wonder if I might . . . that is . . . (*He can't finish it.*)

The others have come to the steps. WENTWORTH *gets down first, and assists* MARY *and* HENRIETTA.

LOUISA: Catch me!

LOUISA jumps from the top step. WENTWORTH *catches her and sets her on the ground, laughing. She immediately runs up the steps again.*

WENTWORTH: No! It's too high!

LOUISA (*laughing*): I am determined, Captain!

WENTWORTH: Louisa, don't be so foolish –

LOUISA turns and jumps before WENTWORTH *is ready. He fails to catch her, and she crumples on the flagstones, banging her head against the step. There is a brief frozen moment; then all is chaos and confusion, and decorum is forgotten.* WENTWORTH *dives to the ground to lift*

LOUISA *in his arms. She is unconscious.* CHARLES *leaps
down from the wall.*

MARY: She is dead!

MARY *grabs hold of* CHARLES, *hysterically.* HENRIET-
TA *faints and is caught by* BENWICK. ANNE *bends over*
LOUISA *and listens for her breath.*

ANNE: No, she breathes!

WENTWORTH (*in despair*): What shall I do?

Their eyes meet across LOUISA'S *limp form. For once it is*
ANNE *who is in control.*

ANNE: Rub her hands, rub her temples!

ANNE *scrabbles in her purse and finds a bottle of smelling
salts. She opens it and holds it under* LOUISA'S *nose; but*
LOUISA *doesn't respond.*

WENTWORTH: Oh God! her father and mother!

ANNE: Fetch a surgeon!

WENTWORTH *is up and running off, leaving* ANNE *to hold*
LOUISA *– but* ANNE *calls him back.*

ANNE: No – Benwick! Benwick will know where to go!

BENWICK *hands* HENRIETTA *to* CHARLES, *and runs off
down the Cobb. A group of curious fishermen are starting
to come towards them.*

CHARLES: Anne! What in heaven's name is to be done?

All eyes, including WENTWORTH'S, *are on* ANNE. *She
stays cool.*

ANNE: Carry her to the Harvilles'.

WENTWORTH: Yes!

ANNE: Gently!

WENTWORTH *picks up* LOUISA *in his arms.*

HARVILLE'S COTTAGE. DAY.

LOUISA *lies unconscious on the sofa in the* HARVILLES'
crowded sitting-room. A SURGEON *bends over her. Also
crowded into the room are* MR *and* MRS HARVILLE, ANNE,

CHARLES, BENWICK, MARY, *a weeping* HENRIETTA, *and*
WENTWORTH, *who sits at a table with his head in his hands.*

ANNE: A message should be sent to Uppercross directly.
And Henrietta should be taken home to her mother.
WENTWORTH: Charles, either you or I must go.
CHARLES: I cannot leave my poor sister.
MRS HARVILLE (*to* SURGEON): Lay her in my bed.

MRS HARVILLE'S BEDROOM. DAY.
A simple bedroom. ANNE *and* MRS HARVILLE *have nearly
finished undressing* LOUISA *and arranging her comfortably in
the bed. They bustle around efficiently.*

HARVILLE'S SITTING-ROOM. DAY.
As ANNE *comes towards the sitting-room, she overhears the
conversation:*

WENTWORTH: I think it should be Anne. No one so capable
as Anne!
ANNE *enters the room.*
WENTWORTH: You will stay, won't you? Stay and nurse
her?
He speaks with gentleness and warmth.
MARY (*weeping*): Why should I go away, instead of Anne?
Anne is nothing to Louisa – I am family! Really, it is too
unkind!
CHARLES: Please, Mary –
MARY: No! Let Anne take Henrietta!
There is nothing to be done. MARY'*s crying;* HENRIET-
TA'*s crying.* CHARLES *looks pleadingly at*
WENTWORTH, *who doesn't like this arrangement at all.*
54

COUNTRYSIDE. NIGHT.
In the curricle, WENTWORTH, HENRIETTA *and* ANNE *drive fast through dark countryside towards Uppercross.* HEN-RIETTA *has cried herself to sleep. The moon is up. It would be a beautiful drive, in different circumstances.* WENTWORTH *and* ANNE *keep glancing sideways at each other; clearly there is something between them that prevents them having a normal conversation.*

WENTWORTH: If only . . .
ANNE: Yes.
    Pause.
WENTWORTH: Anne . . . I regret that . . .
    Another pause. This is hell for them both. WENTWORTH
    finally looks at her, then looks away.
WENTWORTH: Damned foolish. *Damned* foolish!

GREAT HOUSE. NIGHT.
Servants run about with lamps. ANNE *stands in the hall, trying to keep out of the way and not interfere with anybody.*
HENRIETTA *and her distraught Mama are helped upstairs by maids. In his nightshirt and holding a candle,* MR MUSGROVE *strides through the house. It's chaos.*

MUSGROVE: Horses! Horses!
    In all the commotion, nobody notices ANNE.

GREAT HOUSE. NIGHT.
ANNE *walks through a dark passageway next to the courtyard. From outside she hears the clatter of hooves and the shouts of grooms. She looks through a window and is just in time to see* MUSGROVE *and* WENTWORTH *riding off. We get a good look, in the moonlight, at* WENTWORTH, *sitting well on his horse . . . maybe* ANNE's *last sight of him.*

55

GREAT HOUSE. NIGHT.

ANNE *stands alone in the drawing-room, in the dark,*
motionless.

GREAT HOUSE. DAWN.

A grey light breaks over Uppercross. It is pouring with rain. It
thumps against the drawing-room windows. ANNE *sits at the*
piano, and picks out the naval air which WENTWORTH *had*
once tried to demonstrate. Suddenly she is interrupted by the
sound of a horse galloping up to the house. She stops playing.
Outside in the hall, the front door crashes open. CHARLES
bursts into the drawing-room, in a riding cape, his hat-brim
dripping with rain. He's excited.

CHARLES: She'll live!

>*He runs from the room and dashes up the stairs three at a*
>*time, shouting:*

CHARLES: Mama! She is conscious! She will live!

>*C.U.* ANNE. *She is relieved at the news, but at the same*
>*time wondering: 'So what happens now?' Outside, the rain*
>*continues to pour. With* ANNE, *we look through the*
>*window at the gloomy dawn, and dissolve to:*

BATH. DAY.

ANNE's *face seen from outside the window, through lashings of*
rain. The camera moves to reveal that she's now in SIR
WALTER's *grand residence in Camden Place, Bath. Pull out*
further to see the rolling hills of the city.

CAMDEN PLACE. DAY.

ANNE *is in the smart double drawing-room, looking through the*
window. SIR WALTER *is standing nearby, with* ELIZABETH.
A few weeks in Bath have succeeded in changing ELIZABETH's

image: she now wears a dress of extraordinary lavishness. MRS
CLAY *hangs back discreetly.*

MRS CLAY: It always rains in Bath.
　　ANNE *moves into the room.*
SIR WALTER: I am pleased to have you here with us, Anne.
ANNE (*quite surprised*): Thank you, Father.
SIR WALTER: You will make a fourth at dinner. That must
　　be deemed an advantage.

CAMDEN PLACE. DAY.
ANNE, SIR WALTER, ELIZABETH *and* MRS CLAY *at dinner
in the dining-room. The chilly Elliot formality once again in
evidence.*

SIR WALTER: That is the worst of Bath – the dreadful
　　multitude of its ugly women. I do not mean to say that
　　there are no pretty women, but the number of the plain
　　is out of all proportion. I have frequently observed that
　　one handsome face will be followed by thirty, or five
　　and thirty frights. Once as I stood in a shop in Bond
　　Street I counted eighty-seven women go by, one after
　　another, without there being a tolerable face among
　　them! – but then it was a frosty morning, which hardly
　　one woman in a thousand can stand the test of. And as
　　for the men! they are infinitely worse. The streets are
　　full of scarecrows!
ELIZABETH: Mr Elliot is hardly a scarecrow.
SIR WALTER: Mr Elliot is not ill-looking, at all.
　　ANNE *is confused and slightly flabbergasted.*
ANNE: Mr Elliot . . . our cousin?
SIR WALTER: Mr Elliot has been most attentive during our
　　time in Bath. He calls almost every day. He has a most
　　congenial friend, a Colonel Wallis.

57

ANNE: But I thought . . .

ELIZABETH: We may see him yet this afternoon. Then you shall perceive, Anne, what a gentleman he is.

MRS CLAY: And such fine manners!

ANNE: I saw him, in fact, at Lyme.

SIR WALTER: Saw whom?

ANNE: Mr Elliot. We met by chance in Lyme.

ELIZABETH (*condescendingly*): Perhaps it was Mr Elliot.

ANNE: It was.

ELIZABETH (*aggressively*): Well, I do not know. It might have been him, perhaps.

CAMDEN PLACE. DAY.

ANNE, ELIZABETH, MRS CLAY *and* SIR WALTER *in the double drawing-room.* SIR WALTER *reads the paper.*

MRS CLAY: What's the news, Sir Walter?

SIR WALTER: A concert at the Assembly Rooms – to be given in Italian (*He grimaces.*) . . . A display of fireworks . . . But here is news, indeed! Most vital news!
He seems suddenly agitated and uncomfortable.

ELIZABETH: Father?

SIR WALTER: The Dowager Lady Dalrymple and the Honourable Miss Carteret are arrived in Laura Place!

ELIZABETH: Our cousins!

SIR WALTER (*worried*): Will they receive us, do you think?

ELIZABETH: They would not snub us, surely . . . !

SIR WALTER: If it please God, let them not snub us!
The BUTLER *knocks at the door and announces:*

BUTLER: Mr Elliot.

A flurry of excitement. ELLIOT *enters the room, very well-dressed and gracious. He bows low.* ANNE *is curious: why has he suddenly been accepted back into the fold?*

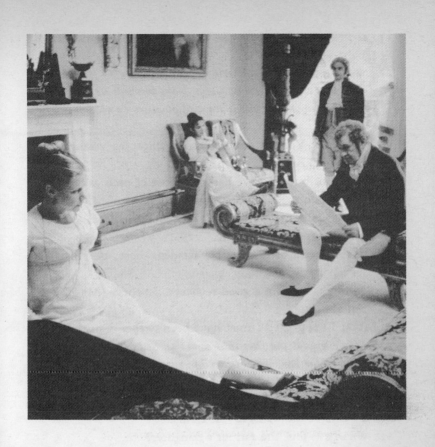

ELLIOT: Good afternoon, Sir Walter. Ladies. I happened to be passing by, and –

SIR WALTER (*warmly*): Come in, come in!
The BUTLER *leaves.* ELLIOT *looks towards* ANNE, *and she blushes as he gives a start of pleasure on recognising her.*

SIR WALTER: You do not know, Mr Elliot, my younger daughter, Anne.

ELLIOT: Oh, but we have had a glimpse of each other, Sir Walter, on the seashore, down at Lyme.
ANNE *and* ELLIOT *smile at each other: he looks attractive, and so does she.*

ELLIOT: I learnt of the terrible accident there, after I had left. Is the young lady. . . ?

ANNE: She is making a good recovery, I believe, Mr Elliot, but slowly.

ELLIOT: I am glad. It must have been deeply disturbing.
ANNE *enjoys the fact that someone, at last, shows some concern for her. The others don't know what they're talking about.*

SIR WALTER: . . . Which young lady, pray?

ANNE: One of the Musgroves. Louisa.

SIR WALTER: Oh, the farmer's daughter?

CATHEDRAL SQUARE. DAY.
ANNE *and* LADY RUSSELL *walk through the cathedral square. The streets are busy and noisy.* ANNE *has been recounting the events in Lyme.*

LADY RUSSELL (*to* ANNE): Mr Elliot? Mr Elliot a guest at Camden Place? But he and your father have not exchanged one word since his most inappropriate marriage.

60

ANNE: He is now a widower, Lady Russell; and shows a
strong desire for a reconciliation.

THE PUMP ROOM. DAY.
ANNE *and* LADY RUSSELL *promenade around the Pump
Room with the fashionable people. Pewter cups of spa water are
dispensed from a fountain in a central alcove by two waiters.*
ANNE *and* LADY RUSSELL *work their way around the vast
room.* LADY RUSSELL *greets a large number of acquaintances.*

ANNE (*continuing*): He holds my father, he says, in high
esteem.
LADY RUSSELL: It is perfectly natural that, at a mature time
of life, Mr Elliot should begin to appreciate the value of
blood and connexion. Has he manners?
ANNE: Very good manners, and correct opinions, and a wide
knowledge of the world.
LADY RUSSELL: This is all most agreeable. The heir-
presumptive reformed, and on good terms with the head
of his family. Most agreeable.
They reach the fountain and drink the water. ANNE *pulls
a face.* LADY RUSSELL *drains her cup.*
ANNE: I suspect Mr Elliot also wishes to be on good terms
with my sister Elizabeth.
LADY RUSSELL: Elizabeth . . . ?
ANNE (*slyly*): Elizabeth is many hours at her dressing-table
when he is expected.
LADY RUSSELL *smiles, amused at* ANNE'*s innocence.*
ANNE *is looking better and better: her hair is lustrous, and
she spends more time on it; her cheeks are rosy; she has put
on a little weight.* LADY RUSSELL *turns to greet an
ancient couple of her acquaintance.*
LADY RUSSELL: Lady Willoughby. Sir Henry. Tell me, did
you attend the Philosophical Society?

62

SIR HENRY: Why yes, Lady Russell.

LADY RUSSELL: And was the resolution carried?

SIR HENRY: It was. The atheists were routed.

LADY WILLOUGHBY: Routed!

> LADY RUSSELL *smiles with satisfaction.* ANNE'S *attention is caught by the entry through the main door of* ADMIRAL *and* MRS CROFT. *They scour the room for people they might know, and seeing* ANNE, *both wave gaily.* ANNE *can't restrain her enthusiasm. She lifts her skirts and runs the length of the Pump Room to greet them.* LADY RUSSELL *is absolutely aghast at this lack of decorum.* ANNE *and the* CROFTS *shake hands, laughing.*

ADMIRAL: Miss Anne!

ANNE: Oh, I am pleased to see *you* here!

MRS CROFT: We are come to improve the Admiral's health.

ANNE: Why, Admiral, what is the problem?

ADMIRAL: Dry land, my dear, dry land; it seems not to agree with me legs.

> *They laugh.*

CAMDEN PLACE. DAY.

Drawing-room. ANNE *is about to enter when she hears a conversation inside being conducted in low voices. Something stops her going in, and, reflected in one of the large mirrors which adorn the walls, she can see* SIR WALTER, ELIZABETH *and* MRS CLAY *in a huddle.*

MRS CLAY: . . . and now that she is settled here, I cannot suppose myself wanted. Oughtn't I perhaps to go home . . . ?

ELIZABETH: There is no reason to do that. I assure you she is nothing to me, compared with you.

SIR WALTER: My dear madam, as yet you have seen nothing of Bath. You must not run away from us now.

ANNE *takes a deep breath and enters the room.*

MRS CLAY (*sweetly*): Good morning.

MRS CLAY *leaves the room.*

SIR WALTER (*very pleased with himself*): We wait this morning, Anne, upon our cousins, the Dowager Lady Dalrymple and the Honourable Miss Carteret; you will accompany us, I hope.

ANNE (*reluctantly*): If you wish it.

ELIZABETH: A Viscountess, she is a Viscountess, and family.

SIR WALTER: Family connexions are always worth preserving. We shall call and be presented. Your looks are greatly improved, Anne; you are less thin in your person, in your cheeks; and your complexion is fresher. What are you using? Gowland's Lotion?

ANNE: No, nothing.

SIR WALTER: I recommend the constant use of Gowland's, during the spring months. Mrs Clay has been using it, and you see what it has done for her: it has quite carried away her freckles.

LAURA PLACE. DAY.

The drawing-room of LADY DALRYMPLE's *grand residence in Laura Place. She is a crotchety old dog and her daughter,* MISS CARTERET, *is a long thin bean-pole of a woman, short-sighted and dull. But they are nobility. A* BUTLER *announces the* ELLIOT *party:*

BUTLER: Sir Walter Elliot, late of Kellynch Hall; Lady Russell; Miss Elizabeth Elliot; Miss Anne Elliot; and Mrs – ? (MRS CLAY *hastily whispers in his ear.*) Mrs Clay.

SIR WALTER, LADY RUSSELL, ELIZABETH, ANNE *and* MRS CLAY *enter the* DALRYMPLE's *drawing-room.*

LADY DALRYMPLE *remains seated.* SIR WALTER *bows low to her, fawning.* LADY DALRYMPLE *looks bored.*

CAMDEN PLACE. NIGHT.
The double drawing-room. SIR WALTER, MRS CLAY, LADY RUSSELL *and* ELIZABETH *play cards at the table. Further off,* ANNE *sits on a sofa with* MR ELLIOT. *She enjoys his company.*

ANNE: My father declared it a notable success. But I can discern no superiority of manner, accomplishment, or understanding in the Dalrymples, and that is all there is to it.

ELLIOT *(with a smile)*: Good company is always worth seeking. They may be nothing in themselves; but they will collect good company around them.

ANNE: My idea of good company, Mr Elliot, is the fellowship of clever, well-informed people, who have a great deal of conversation, and a liberality of ideas; that is what I call good company.

ELLIOT: That is not good company. That is the best. Good company requires only birth, education and manners, and with regard to education it is not very particular. (ANNE *shakes her head.*) My dear cousin, the Dalrymples will move in the first set in Bath this winter, and as rank is rank, your being known to be related will be highly advantageous.

ANNE: I perceive your value for rank and connexion to be greater than mine.

ELLIOT *(laughing)*: Not at all. You are simply too proud to admit it.

ANNE: Am I?

ELLIOT: Yes. I think we are very alike.

ANNE *(smiling)*: Are we? In what respect?

ELLIOT: In one respect, I am certain. (*Softly*.) We both feel that every opportunity for your father to mix in the best society may be of use in diverting his thoughts from those who are beneath him.

With that, he glances at MRS CLAY. ANNE *does not dislike him for it.*

ANNE: You presume to know me very well, Mr Elliot.

ELLIOT: In my heart, I know you . . . intimately.

CAMDEN PLACE. DAY.

ANNE, SIR WALTER, ELIZABETH *and* MRS CLAY *at breakfast in the dining-room.*

SIR WALTER (*furious*): Westgate Buildings! And who is this invalid that you visit in Westgate Buildings?

ANNE: A Mrs Smith.

SIR WALTER: A Mrs Smith.

ANNE: A widow.

SIR WALTER: A widow Mrs Smith. And what is her attraction? That she is old and sickly. Upon my word, Miss Anne Elliot, you have the most extraordinary taste! Everything that revolts other people is inviting to you.

ANNE: She is a former schoolfellow of mine, Father, and I am engaged to spend this afternoon with her.

SIR WALTER (*a card in his hand*): But Lady Dalrymple's invitation is most pressing. Surely you may put off this old person till tomorrow.

ANNE: It is the only afternoon for some time which will at once suit her and myself.

SIR WALTER: And you would snub Lady Dalrymple for a Mrs Smith, lodging in Westgate Buildings? You would prefer an everyday Mrs Smith to your own family

connexions among the nobility of England and Ireland!
Mrs Smith, such a name!

At this point MRS CLAY *thinks it tactful to slip quietly out*
of the room. ANNE *sees her go, and this stiffens her resolve.*

SIR WALTER: Now, will you, or will you not, accompany us
to the tea-party at our cousins, the Dalrymples?

ANNE (*flushed with anger*): No, sir, I will not. I have a prior
engagement, with Mrs Smith – who is not the only
widow in Bath, with little to live on, and no surname of
dignity.

It is SIR WALTER'*s turn to colour.* ELIZABETH *says*
'*Oh!*' *and swishes out after her friend.*

WESTGATE BUILDINGS. DAY.

MRS SMITH'*s lodgings: a small parlour, with a dark bedroom*
off. MRS SMITH *is in a dilapidated wheelchair. She is the same*
age as ANNE, *but a hard life has left its ravages on her face.*
ANNE *sits by a tiny fire, looking very healthy and happy in*
comparison. NURSE ROOKE *straightens the rug over* MRS
SMITH'*s legs, and prepares her medication.*

ANNE: But do you not suffer from melancholy?

MRS SMITH (*laughing*): How could I be melancholy, when
you are come to visit?

ANNE: Can you walk at all?

MRS SMITH: No. But I will not let sickness ruin my spirits.

ANNE: Did your husband leave you any money?

MRS SMITH: Very little – his affairs had utterly collapsed.
And it is all spent on Nurse Rooke; who, besides
carrying me into the Hot Bath, brings me my one source
of consolation: delicious gossip from the world outside.

ANNE (*laughs*): So you are a spy, Nurse Rooke?

NURSE ROOKE: I keep my ears open, that's all.

MRS SMITH: And what have you heard of my friend here?

67

NURSE ROOKE: Well, I know her cousin Mr Elliot thinks terribly highly of her.

ANNE: How on earth do you know that?

NURSE ROOKE: I attend on Colonel Wallis's wife, Miss, who is indisposed with a baby; and she says that Colonel Wallis says that Mr Elliot says that –

ANNE: That's enough!

MRS SMITH: You see, Anne? There are no secrets in Bath.

MILSOM STREET. DAY.

ANNE *walks home through the centre of Bath with* ADMIRAL CROFT. *They saunter along Milsom Street. The* ADMIRAL *is constantly saying 'how d'ye do' to naval acquaintances.*

ADMIRAL: Do you remember my brother-in-law, Frederick?

ANNE: Yes.

ADMIRAL: Well, we thought he was to marry Louisa Musgrove. He was courting her week after week. The only wonder was, what were they waiting for? – till the business at Lyme happened; then it was clear that they must wait till her brain was set to right. But now the matter has taken the strangest turn of all: for Frederick has removed to Shropshire, and the young lady, instead of being to marry *him*, is to marry James Benwick. You know James Benwick.

ANNE *has to stand still for a moment.*

ANNE: I am a little acquainted with Captain Benwick, yes.

ADMIRAL: Well, she is to marry him.

ANNE: I confess I am amazed!

ADMIRAL: Aye, it is certainly unforeseen. But it's true. We have it in a letter from Frederick himself.

ANNE: But their minds are so dissimilar!

ADMIRAL: Yes, but they were thrown together several weeks; and Louisa, just recovering from illness, would be in an interesting state, would she not? (*There is a twinkle in his eye.*)

ANNE: No doubt Louisa will learn to be an enthusiast for Scott and Lord Byron.

ADMIRAL: Nay, that is learnt already. (*They laugh.*)

ANNE: Of course! They fell in love over poetry! (*More laughter.*)

ADMIRAL: So Frederick is unshackled, and free.

ANNE *has to stop laughing and stare at the ground to hide her confused feelings. She takes the* ADMIRAL*'s arm again and they walk on.*

ANNE: And is he bitter?

ADMIRAL: Not at all, not at all – his letter is sanguine – there is barely an oath from beginning to end.

ANNE *hides her smile.*

ADMIRAL: You would not guess, from his way of writing, that he had ever thought of this Musgrove girl for himself. Poor Frederick! Now he must begin all over again, with somebody else.

MOLLAND'S CAKE SHOP. DAY.
It's raining on Milsom Street. ELIZABETH, MRS CLAY *and* ANNE *are sheltering in Molland's. The shop has a long counter and is thronged with people. The ladies stand near the window.* ANNE *stares out, distant.*

ELIZABETH: Oh, this rain!

MRS CLAY: I am sure Mr Elliot will return in a moment.

ELIZABETH: I think Molland's marzipan is as fine as any in Bath, do not you, Penelope?

MRS CLAY: Oh it is, it is, quite as fine.

ELLIOT *comes in.*

ELLIOT: I have found Lady Dalrymple's carriage. She will be pleased to convey you home. She has, alas, room only for two.

MRS CLAY: It is no trouble to me to walk.

ELIZABETH: Nonsense. You have a cold. Anne will walk.

MRS CLAY: Really, I am content. (*to* ELLIOT.) You might show me that parasol that you mentioned.

ELLIOT *and* MRS CLAY'*s eyes meet for a second.*

ELIZABETH: You will ruin your shoes. Anne has thick boots. (*Firmly.*) Mr Elliot, would you be so kind?

ELLIOT: I should be delighted to escort Miss Anne.

ELIZABETH: Then it is settled. Please tell the coachman we are ready.

ELLIOT *steps outside once more.* ANNE *is uninterested in the proceedings. She's still looking out of the window. She sees* CAPTAIN WENTWORTH *striding down the street, away from the cake shop. Her heart thumps. She goes white.*

MRS CLAY: Miss Anne? Are you unwell?

ANNE: I will just take a breath of air.

She heads towards the door. As she gets there, WENTWORTH *unexpectedly enters Molland's.* ANNE *tries to return to her place, but the crowd makes it impossible. She and* WENTWORTH *suddenly face each other. For the first time, she has a slight advantage over him.*

ANNE: Good morning, Captain Wentworth.

WENTWORTH: Miss Elliot.

ANNE: So, you are come to Bath?

WENTWORTH (*embarrassed, and lost for words*): Well, yes, I am.

ANNE: And how do you like it?

WENTWORTH (*looking directly at her*): Bath? I have yet to see it.

ANNE *looks across the room towards* ELIZABETH. *She is ashamed to see that* ELIZABETH *will not recognise* WENTWORTH; *she pointedly turns away.*

WENTWORTH: Your family. . . ?

ANNE: Yes. . . ?

WENTWORTH: Are they in health?

ANNE: They are.

WENTWORTH: And you? Are you, er – in health?

WENTWORTH *is still flustered, and not his usual confident self.* ANNE *smiles at him.*

ANNE: I am very well indeed, thank you, Captain.

LADY DALRYMPLE's *carriage now draws up outside the door, and her* COACHMAN *enters Molland's.*

COACHMAN: Lady Dalrymple's carriage, for the Miss Elliots!

ELIZABETH (*loudly*): That's us.

ELIZABETH *and* MRS CLAY *head ostentatiously for the door, and leave, without a 'goodbye' to* ANNE.

WENTWORTH: You're not going too?

ANNE (*smiles*): There is no room. I shall walk.

WENTWORTH: But it's raining!

ANNE: Oh, very little. Nothing that I regard. I like to walk.

WENTWORTH: Though I got here only yesterday, I've already armed myself for Bath. (*He shows her a new umbrella.*) Please, take it.

ANNE *takes the umbrella.* ELLIOT *comes in at that moment.* ANNE *sees that* WENTWORTH *recognises him immediately: a dark look passes over his face.* ELLIOT *treats* ANNE *with familiarity.*

ELLIOT: I am so sorry to have kept you waiting. Shall we set off? The rain has eased.

ELLIOT *offers her his arm. He has his own umbrella.* ANNE *hands* WENTWORTH's *back to him.*

ANNE: Good morning, Captain.

CAMDEN PLACE. DAY.

Rain. From outside, we see ANNE *looking wistfully through the drawing-room window. A moment later,* ELLIOT *appears behind her, and speaks to her. He takes her arm gently, and they turn back into the room.*

ASSEMBLY ROOMS. EVENING.

ANNE *walks slowly through the throng of people entering the Assembly Rooms, looking for Wentworth.*

ASSEMBLY ROOMS. NIGHT.

In the Octagon Room, the main foyer of the Assembly Rooms. People are arriving for the concert. SIR WALTER, ELIZABETH, ANNE *and* MRS CLAY, *dressed in their best gear, are standing by one of the four great fires;* ANNE's *hair is now prettily and fashionably arranged. Then* CAPTAIN WENTWORTH *walks in alone. He gives a little bow to the party and prepares to pass on, but* ANNE, *her eyes suddenly bright, takes a few steps forward to intercept him.*

ANNE: How d'ye do, Captain?

WENTWORTH: Well, thank you, Miss Elliot.

ANNE: You have come for the concert?

WENTWORTH: No, I came for a lecture on navigation. Am I in the wrong place?

    ANNE *laughs. A pause. Though they are both uncomfortable, she stands in his way, and won't let him pass. She hears whispering between* SIR WALTER *and* ELIZABETH, *who are standing behind her. So far they have ignored* WENTWORTH *completely. But now* SIR WALTER *bows.* WENTWORTH *returns it, and receives a slight curtsy from* ELIZABETH. *This lifts* ANNE's *spirits, and encourages* WENTWORTH.

WENTWORTH: I've hardly seen you since our day at Lyme. That was a wretched day! I'm afraid you must have suffered from the shock – more so from its not overpowering you at the time.

ANNE: I do not think I was in danger of suffering from not being overpowered, thank you, Captain.

WENTWORTH (*smiles*): But when you had the presence of mind to send Benwick for a surgeon, I bet you had little idea of the consequences.

ANNE: No, I had none. But I hope it will be a very happy match.

WENTWORTH: I, too, wish them luck. They have no difficulties to contend with at home, no opposition, no caprice, no delays . . . And yet . . . Louisa Musgrove is a very amiable, sweet-tempered girl, and not unin-telligent; but Benwick – he's something more. He's a clever man, a reading man – and I do view his – I mean that he – suddenly attaching himself to her like that! A man in his situation! With a broken heart! Phoebe Harville was wonderful, and he was devoted to her. A man does not recover from such a devotion to such a woman! – he ought not – he does not.

To ANNE, *the buzz of the people now milling round the Octagon Room has melted away; all she can hear is his voice. She feels a hundred things at once; her pulse races. She still doesn't want to let him go.*

ANNE: Did you stay long at Lyme?

WENTWORTH *breathes deeply and pulls himself together.*

WENTWORTH: About a fortnight. The country round about is very fine. I walked and rode a great deal.

ANNE: I should very much like to see it again.

WENTWORTH (*surprised*): Would you? I'd have thought – I mean, the distress! – too painful.

73

ANNE: But when the pain is over . . . I have travelled so little, every fresh place is interesting to me. One day I should like to see Lyme again.

WENTWORTH: . . . It was my doing, solely mine. Louisa would not have been obstinate if I had not been weak.

The crowd parts to admit LADY DALRYMPLE *and* MISS CARTERET, *and a general murmur goes up –* 'Lady Dalrymple, Lady Dalrymple.'

WENTWORTH: Anne – I have never –

Then they have to break apart, as SIR WALTER, ELIZABETH *and* MRS CLAY *step forward to greet* LADY DALRYMPLE. *It is necessary that* ANNE *should do so too; after she has curtsied to* LADY DALRYMPLE *and* MISS CARTERET, *she turns back, to find that* WENTWORTH *has gone.*

CONCERT HALL. NIGHT

In the concert hall is a chamber orchestra and an Italian singer. The audience are arranged on benches. As the music plays, ANNE *is sharing the concert programme with the man seated next to her. We don't see who it is, at first, as* ANNE *translates in a whisper the Italian text of the song.*

ANNE: . . . and after they have done this their two hearts will, ah, combine in eternal union. That is the literal meaning of the words; to give the sense would not I think be proper. And besides, I am a poor Italian scholar.

Pull out to reveal that ANNE *is seated next to* MR ELLIOT.

ELLIOT: Yes, I see you are. I see you have only enough knowledge of the language to translate it at sight into clear, comprehensible English. You need not say

74

anything more of your ignorance – here is complete
proof.

ANNE (*smiling*): Well, I should be sorry to be examined by a
real proficient, Mr Elliot.

ELLIOT: You are too modest. The world is not aware of half
your accomplishments.

ANNE: This is too much flattery.

ELLIOT: I do not think I could ever flatter you enough.

ANNE *is worrying about how to respond to this when the
music stops for the interval. There is polite applause.
ANNE hears her father, sitting behind her with* LADY
DALRYMPLE.

SIR WALTER: Yes, a well-looking man, a very well-looking
man.

LADY DALRYMPLE (*peering across the room*): A very fine
young man indeed! More air than one often sees in
Bath. Irish, I dare say.

SIR WALTER: Captain Wentworth of the Navy. A bowing
acquaintance. His sister married my tenant in
Somersetshire.

ANNE *follows where they are looking and sees* WENT-
WORTH *across the floor, standing among a cluster of men.
As her eyes fall on him, he – who has been looking at her –
immediately looks away. She feels the presence of* ELLIOT
at her side, leaning into her, his face only inches from hers.
WENTWORTH *suddenly breaks from his group and heads
rather forcefully for the door.*

ELLIOT: Do you follow my meaning, Anne? Or must I
translate for you?

ANNE: Please excuse me for one moment.

ANNE *stands and with difficulty makes her way out of the
seats. She cuts off* WENTWORTH *just before he reaches the
exit.*

ANNE: Oh, Captain, are you leaving already?

WENTWORTH: Yes.

ANNE: But the music is good, is it not?

WENTWORTH: I do not know – or care.

ANNE: Will you –

WENTWORTH: What? (*He glares at her, crossly.*)

ANNE: This is too sudden!

WENTWORTH: Is it? Oh.

ANNE (*thinking how warm he had been, half an hour before*):
But what is the matter with you?

WENTWORTH: Nothing at all. Nothing.

ELLIOT: Miss Elliot.

> ELLIOT *is at her shoulder, touching her lightly on the arm.*
> ANNE *turns with an expression of undisguised alarm.*
> WENTWORTH *goes very frosty.*

ELLIOT: You must come, to explain the Italian again. Miss
Carteret is anxious to know what is being sung.

> ANNE *looks across at* MISS CARTERET, *who is smiling
> through yellow teeth, and holding aloft her programme.*

WENTWORTH: Good night.

ANNE: The next song is very beautiful – very beautiful love
song – is that not worth your staying for?

WENTWORTH (*barks*): No, there is nothing worth my
staying for.

> WENTWORTH *leaves fast. The orchestra starts up the
> next song.* ANNE *turns to find* ELLIOT *smiling at her.*

ELLIOT: Anne, it's beginning.

> *He leads her back to her place. The music soars.*

CAMDEN PLACE. DAY.
Next day. A carriage pulls up outside Camden Place, and
CHARLES *and* MARY MUSGROVE *alight from it.* MARY
stares up at the grand house, clutching CHARLES's *arm in
rapturous excitement.*

CAMDEN PLACE. DAY.

ANNE, ELIZABETH, MRS CLAY *and* SIR WALTER *are in the*
double drawing-room with CHARLES *and* MARY.

ELIZABETH (*somewhat alarmed*): But, Mary dear, where are
    you staying?
MARY: We are at the White Hart, with Mrs Musgrove, and
    Henrietta, and Captain Harville – you remember him,
    Anne, from Lyme.
ELIZABETH (*much warmer*): Come and see upstairs!
SIR WALTER: And what brings old Mrs Musgrove up to
    Bath?
MARY: She is come to buy wedding-clothes for Henrietta
    and her sister! It is so exciting, it makes me feel giddy! A
    double wedding!

THE WHITE HART. DAY.
A large drawing-room taken by the MUSGROVE *party, with a*
window overlooking the entrance to the Pump Room. MARY *sits*
at it, watching the comings and goings in the street. ANNE *sits*
with HENRIETTA *and* MRS MUSGROVE *and a* MILLINER,
looking through boxes and boxes of ribbons and lace.

MRS MUSGROVE: What do you think for Louisa's hair,
    Anne? This? Or this?
HENRIETTA: Louisa is become so severe, Mama, I wonder
    she will want a ribbon in her hair at all. Give her a book
    of verse to hold, instead.
    The door opens to admit CHARLES, *who brings with him*
    CAPTAIN HARVILLE *and* CAPTAIN WENTWORTH.
CHARLES: Look who I found, Mama.
MRS MUSGROVE: Captain Wentworth! How splendid!
    The men bow to the ladies and all say their 'good
    mornings'. HARVILLE *smiles warmly at* ANNE.

77

WENTWORTH *seems to be keeping his distance from her.*
He's still jealous.

CHARLES: And I've done something, Mama, that you will
like. I've been to the Theatre Royal, and secured a box
for tomorrow night. Ain't I a good boy?

HENRIETTA *and* MRS MUSGROVE *are thrilled.*

MRS MUSGROVE: Anne, you will accompany us, I do hope?

ANNE: I am obliged to you, Mrs Musgrove, but I cannot.
There is an evening party at Camden Place, to which I
understand you shall all be invited.

CHARLES: Pshaw! What's an evening party?

ANNE: If it depended only on me, Charles, I assure you I
should prefer the theatre. But I have an obligation to my
family.

MRS MUSGROVE: Then we shall go another time, when you
are free to join us.

ANNE *acknowledges* MRS MUSGROVE *with a smile, and*
moves away to sit on the sofa. WENTWORTH *saunters*
indirectly towards her, as if tacking into the wind.

WENTWORTH: Perhaps you've not been long enough in
Bath to learn to enjoy these parties they give.

ANNE: They mean nothing to me. Those who hold them
believe the theatre to be beneath their dignity. But I am
no card player.

WENTWORTH: No, you never were, were you?

MARY *suddenly calls to* ANNE *from her window-seat.*

MARY: Anne! There is Mrs Clay, I am sure, standing under
the colonnade, and a gentleman with her. Bless my soul,
it's Mr Elliot!

ANNE: No, it cannot be Mr Elliot, he is gone out of Bath for
two days, to stay with his friends at Combe Park.

ANNE *glances at* WENTWORTH, *who is now looking*
coolly at her. She is embarrassed to seem to know so much
about ELLIOT's *business.*

MARY: Upon my word, I think I may be supposed to know my own cousin! Come and look!

Reluctantly, ANNE *goes to the window. Sure enough, she sees* ELLIOT *and* MRS CLAY *in earnest conversation on the street below.* ELLIOT *touches* MRS CLAY *lightly on the arm, and they smile, and rapidly go their separate ways.* ANNE *frowns.*

MARY: Was it not Mr Elliot?

ANNE *turns back into the room.* WENTWORTH *is still watching her, even more jealous. She cannot meet his eye.*

PUMP ROOM. DAY.

ANNE *and* LADY RUSSELL, *on their usual circuit. But this time* LADY RUSSELL *is pursuing* ANNE, *who strides away from her with a determined expression.* LADY RUSSELL *won't talk too loudly for fear of being overheard by her acquaintances, so she has to scurry to get up close to* ANNE's *ear; and* ANNE *keeps breaking away and moving forward through the crowd.*

LADY RUSSELL: You must see the aptness of the match! (ANNE *shakes her head stubbornly.*) You would step into your dear mother's shoes, as mistress of Kellynch! Anybody capable of thought must approve it!

ANNE: He is very charming, but my instinct says –

LADY RUSSELL: Instinct? This is no time for instinct! Look at the facts. The present Mr Elliot is the most eligible gentleman you are ever likely to –

ANNE *suddenly stops and squares up to her.*

ANNE: But what of the past Mr Elliot? Why has his character altered so profoundly? Why do I feel I know him so little?

LADY RUSSELL: You do not know him?

ANNE: Oh, he is charming, he is clever – but I have never seen any burst of feeling, any warmth of fury or delight!

79

LADY RUSSELL: You will come to know him.

ANNE: That is not what I want.

> LADY RUSSELL *is taken aback by* ANNE's *firmness. A* FOOTMAN *approaches them and speaks to* ANNE.

FOOTMAN: Miss Elliot? There is a gentleman of the Navy wishes to speak privately with you. Concerning Kellynch Hall in Somerset, he says.

ANNE (*brightening*): It must be the Admiral. Excuse me, please.

> ANNE *leaves the Pump Room with the* FOOTMAN, *through a side door.* LADY RUSSELL *watches her for a second, but is almost immediately engaged in conversation by another acquaintance.*

ANTE-ROOM. DAY.

The FOOTMAN *opens the door for her, and* ANNE *emerges from the Pump Room into a little ante-room, where there are chairs lined up against the wall. But sitting there, instead of the Admiral, is* WENTWORTH. *He stands and looks embarrassed as he bows to* ANNE. *She hastily looks around for an escape, but there is none – the* FOOTMAN *has closed the door and disappeared. No one else is present.* ANNE *is alone with* WENTWORTH. *He's very uncomfortable.*

WENTWORTH: I have a commission from my Admiral, and I must discharge it, though you may think me impertinent. But remember, I speak for him. The Admiral is aware that everything is settled for a union between Mr Elliot and yourself.

> ANNE *gasps.*

WENTWORTH: It has occurred to the Admiral that when you are married, it might be your wish to return to Kellynch Hall, your family seat. And I am charged to tell you that – if this should be the case – the Admiral

will cancel his lease, and he and my sister will find
themselves another place. There, I've done my duty.
Do you wish it? All you have to do is give me a yes or a
no, and we are both released.

He waits for a reply. ANNE *is thoroughly unnerved.*

ANNE: He is too kind, but . . .

WENTWORTH: Just say it, yes or no.

ANNE (*angrily*): Why is everyone assuming that—

> ANNE *hears the door, and turns to see* LADY RUSSELL
> *entering the room.* ANNE *and* WENTWORTH *stand stock-
> still as* LADY RUSSELL *approaches them slowly, con-
> quering her evident surprise at finding* WENTWORTH
> *here.*

LADY RUSSELL: Captain Wentworth.

WENTWORTH: Lady Russell.

> *A heavy pause.* LADY RUSSELL *looks pointedly at*
> ANNE, *who's still fuming.* ANNE *suddenly turns on her
> heel and leaves the room.*

LADY RUSSELL: You have an extraordinary ability to
discompose my friend, sir.

WENTWORTH: You have an extraordinary ability to
influence her, ma'am, for which I find it hard to forgive
you.

LADY RUSSELL: If persuasion has been exercised, remember that it has been on the side of safety, not of risk. You
have had good fortune, but that was not to be foreseen.
I act in Anne's best interest. I care for her more than for
anyone else in the world.

> *They hold each other's eye.* LADY RUSSELL *suddenly
> realises that* WENTWORTH *feels the same way about*
> ANNE. LADY RUSSELL*'s expression softens slightly; the
> merest hint of a smile plays on her face.*

WESTGATE BUILDINGS. DAY.

Next day. ANNE *enters Westgate Buildings, giving some coins to an old* BEGGAR *who sits on the steps.*

WESTGATE BUILDINGS. DAY.

ANNE *sits with* MRS SMITH. NURSE ROOKE *busies herself around the room.*

ANNE: Oh, why does the whole town suffer this dreadful misapprehension, that I shall marry him?

MRS SMITH: . . . Well, shan't you?

ANNE: No!

> MRS SMITH *and* NURSE ROOKE *exchange a glance, and* MRS SMITH *decides to speak her mind.*

MRS SMITH: I have to say I am relieved to hear it.

ANNE: Relieved? Why?

MRS SMITH: Because . . . did you never wonder why a man who for years had held the honour of your family as cheap as dirt, who had not the slightest interest in the Baronetcy or the Kellynch estate, should suddenly show such interest?

ANNE: What do you know . . . ?

> NURSE ROOKE *looks at* MRS SMITH. MRS SMITH *nods to her: 'Speak.'*

NURSE ROOKE: I was at Colonel Wallis's yesterday. I chanced to hear him complain to his wife that Mr Elliot required another loan.

ANNE: But he is rich!

MRS SMITH: He was rich. He has lost it. His style of life is a sham. He lives on borrowed money.

ANNE: Are you saying he pays his attentions to me because – ?

MRS SMITH: He wants the title. He wants the land. He heard of your sister's friend, Mrs Clay –

NURSE ROOKE: – that she's hoping, perhaps, to become the next Lady Elliot –

MRS SMITH: – and who knows, to provide Sir Walter with a son . . . ?

ANNE: An heir . . .

MRS SMITH: So if he marries you, he gains some footing in the family, and exerts his influence on your father –

NURSE ROOKE: – and keeps his inheritance.

ANNE: But why did you say nothing of this before?

MRS SMITH: We have only just learnt it.

ANNE: How despicable . . . !

WESTGATE BUILDINGS. DAY.
ANNE *leaves Westgate Buildings with her mind in turmoil, struggling to digest what she's just heard.*

THE WHITE HART. DAY.
In the MUSGROVES' *drawing-room are* MRS MUSGROVE, MRS CROFT, HARVILLE *and* WENTWORTH. WENTWORTH *sits at a writing-table in the centre of the room, composing a letter.* MRS MUSGROVE *is talking to* MRS CROFT *as* ANNE *enters.*

ANNE: Good morning, Mrs Musgrove. Good morning, Mrs Croft.
She acknowledges the men, and HARVILLE, *standing at the window, returns it; but* WENTWORTH *seems too intent on his letter to notice her at all.*

MRS MUSGROVE: They are all gone shopping, Anne; but Henrietta has given me strict instructions to keep you here till they return. Please come and sit with us. (*To* MRS CROFT.) And so, ma'am, all things considered, as Henry Hayter was wild about it, and my daughter pretty near as bad, we thought let them marry at once, and make the best of it. At any rate, said I to papa, it will be better than a long engagement. There is nothing I so abominate for young people as a long engagement! ANNE *looks towards* WENTWORTH. *His back is to her, but he has stopped writing, and sits with his pen poised, immobile, just breathing.* ANNE *looks to* HARVILLE. *He smiles and inclines his head: 'Come over here.'* ANNE *gets up and joins him at the window. He shows her a miniature portrait which he has in his hand.*

HARVILLE: Do you know who that is?

ANNE: Captain Benwick.

HARVILLE: Yes. But it wasn't done for Louisa Musgrove. This was drawn at the Cape, for my poor sister. And now I have the charge of getting it set for another! It's too much for me, I confess. So he (*Indicating* WENTWORTH, *who is just within earshot.*) undertakes it; he is writing instructions to the frame-makers now. Poor Phoebe! She would not have forgotten him so soon. It was not in her nature.

ANNE: It would not be in the nature of any woman who truly loved.

HARVILLE (*smiles*): Do you claim that for your sex?

ANNE (*smiles*): We do not forget you as soon as you forget us. We live at home, quiet, confined, and our feelings prey upon us. You always have business of some sort or other, to take you back into the world.

HARVILLE: But that does not apply to Benwick. The peace turned him on shore at the very moment, and he's been living in our family circle ever since.

ANNE: So if the change is not from outward circumstances, it must be from within; it must be nature, man's nature, which has affected Captain Benwick.

HARVILLE: No, no, it is not man's nature. I will not allow it to be any more man's nature than woman's, to be

84

inconstant, and forget those they love, or have loved. I believe the reverse. I believe in –

A slight noise makes them look towards WENTWORTH.
He has dropped his pen on the floor. Now he bends to pick it up.

HARVILLE: Have you finished your letter?

WENTWORTH: Not quite. A few lines more.

HARVILLE (*smiling at* ANNE): Let me just observe that all histories are against you, all stories, prose and verse. I don't think I ever opened a book in my life which did not have something to say on woman's fickleness.

ANNE: But they were all written by men.

HARVILLE (*laughs*): I suppose so, yes. – If I could only make you understand what a man suffers when he takes a last look at his wife and children, and watches the boat that he has sent them off in, as long as it's in sight, and then turns away and says, 'God knows whether we'll ever meet again!' If I could only show you the glow of his soul when he does see them once more; when, coming back after a twelvemonth perhaps, and obliged to put into another port, he calculates how soon he can get them there, pretending to deceive himself, and saying, 'They cannot be here till such a day,' but all the while hoping for them twelve hours sooner, and seeing them arrive at last, as if heaven had given them wings . . . !

ANNE: I believe you capable of everything great and good, so long as – if I may – so long as the woman you love lives, and lives for you. All the privilege I claim for my own sex – and it is not a very enviable one, you need not covet it – is that of loving longest, when all hope is gone.

WENTWORTH *has at times during this debate been listening intently, and at times writing fast. Now* MRS CROFT *rises to take her leave.*

MRS CROFT: Here, Frederick, you and I part company, I believe; but tonight we may have the pleasure of all meeting again, (*to* ANNE.) at your party.

WENTWORTH (*sealing the letter*): Harville, if you are ready, I am at your service.

HARVILLE: Good morning, Miss Elliot. And God bless.

ANNE: Good morning.

MRS CROFT: Good morning.

MRS CROFT, HARVILLE and WENTWORTH all leave together. WENTWORTH neither looks nor speaks to ANNE. She stands forlornly when they are gone.

MRS MUSGROVE: Now where on earth can Henrietta and Mary have taken themselves off to?

The door opens and WENTWORTH returns.

WENTWORTH: I beg your pardon, Mrs Musgrove, I have left my umbrella.

He comes back to the writing-table, which ANNE is still standing near, takes up his umbrella, and, having made sure she is watching, draws out a letter from under a pile of papers, laying it on the table for her. Then he leaves fast.

MRS MUSGROVE: Good day, Captain Wentworth.

WENTWORTH: Ma'am.

MRS MUSGROVE busies herself at her table. ANNE picks up the letter, and sees the inscription on the envelope: 'A.E.' She turns away, and opens it, and reads. Her face conveys a blizzard of emotions: everything that we have seen her go through so far is contained in her reading of this letter.

WENTWORTH: (*V.O.*) I can listen no longer in silence. I must speak to you by such means as are within my reach. You have pierced my soul. I am half agony, half hope. Tell me not that I am too late; that such precious feelings are gone for ever. I offer myself to you with a heart even more your own than when you almost broke it eight years and a half ago. Dare not say that man forgets sooner than woman, that his love has an earlier death. I have loved none but you. Unjust I may have been, weak and resentful I may have been, but never inconstant. You alone have brought me to Bath. For you alone I think and plan. Have you not seen this? Can you fail to have understood my wishes? I must go; but I shall return and follow your party as soon as possible. A word, a look, will be enough to decide whether I enter your father's house this evening, or never.

As she finishes, hardly able to breathe, MARY, HEN-RIETTA *and* CHARLES *come in, full of beans, and greet* MRS MUSGROVE. ANNE *sinks into a chair, looking pale and ill. They notice her condition.*

CHARLES: Anne! Is something the matter?

MRS MUSGROVE: Oh, Anne! Look at you!

ANNE: I feel a little faint. – I will go home, Mrs Musgrove, if I may.

MRS MUSGROVE: By all means, my dear, go home directly and take care of yourself, so you may be fit for this evening. Charles, ring and order a chair.

ANNE: No! – I assure you, Mrs Musgrove, I am well able to walk.

UNION STREET. DAY.

CHARLES *accompanies* ANNE *on to the street. Her eyes dart around, expecting to see* WENTWORTH *at any moment. But he doesn't show. She starts to panic.*

ANNE: Charles, I want you to assure Captain Harville and Captain Wentworth that we hope to see them both tonight.

CHARLES: It was understood, I am sure it was understood.

87

ANNE: No, I do not think it *was* understood. They must come, do you hear? You will see them again this morning. Do promise me you will mention it.

CHARLES: You may mention it yourself.

He indicates WENTWORTH, *who is standing a few paces in front of them. They approach him. His eyes are locked on* ANNE'S. ANNE *returns his gaze, and gives him a tiny smile, mainly with her eyes.* CHARLES *seems a little agitated.*

CHARLES: Which way are you going, Frederick?

WENTWORTH: I hardly know.

CHARLES: Are you going near Camden Place? Because if you are, I shall have no scruple in asking you to give Anne your arm to her father's door. She is rather done for this morning; and I, d'you see, am eager to be at the gun-smith's – he promised me the sight of a capital gun he is just going to send off, a good deal like that double-barrel of mine which you once shot with.

WENTWORTH: I think I have time, Charles, to take her.

CHARLES: I thank you!

And CHARLES *is gone.* WENTWORTH *turns to* ANNE. *He gazes at her for a long time, and gently takes her hand.*

WENTWORTH: I tried to forget you. I thought I had.

ANNE *is almost crying with happiness and relief. She gives him a look meaning: 'I was the same.' They hear a noise, which startles them. Looking up, they see on the street a circus troupe, banging drums and blowing bugles to advertise their show. There are jugglers, acrobats, fire-eaters and so on, all processing down the hill into the town, with a large crowd following, laughing and cheering.*

Slowly, WENTWORTH *bends to kiss* ANNE *lightly on the lips.*

BATH. DAY.
In the foreground, we see the circus troupe, who appear to be
Italian. In the background ANNE *and* WENTWORTH, *arm in*
arm, walk slowly up the hill towards Camden Place, talking
happily.

CAMDEN PLACE. NIGHT.
The ELLIOTS' *card party in the well-lighted drawing-rooms.*
Present are: SIR WALTER, LADY RUSSELL, ELIZABETH,
MRS CLAY, MARY, CHARLES, MRS MUSGROVE,
HENRIETTA, ADMIRAL CROFT, MRS CROFT, LADY
DALRYMPLE, MISS CARTERET *and* MR ELLIOT. *Cards are*
played. ANNE *looks radiant as she moves confidently through*
the room. She passes ELIZABETH, *who whispers in her ear:*

ELIZABETH: When Captain Wentworth comes, do not
    monopolise him. It is a very bad habit of yours.
    ELIZABETH *smiles sweetly.* ANNE *glides on, biting her lip*
    to prevent herself from grinning. She overhears in passing
    ADMIRAL CROFT *speaking to* CHARLES:
ADMIRAL CROFT: Aye, Bonaparte's got off Elba, and raised
    an army in France. (*Quite cheerfully.*) It seems there is
    to be another war.
    ANNE *moves on. A hand grips her arm. It is* LADY
    RUSSELL'S.
LADY RUSSELL: When you make a decision, Anne, you
    must stick with it. There is no going back. At your age I
    found out what *I* wanted, and I made a decision to
    marry, and I am married till I die. I hope, one day, to
    see you do the same.
ANNE: I hope so too.
    She moves on. ELLIOT *is there.*
ELLIOT: Miss Elliot, may we speak a moment?
    He guides her to a sofa, and they sit.
90

ELLIOT: Have you thought any further about my offer?

ANNE: What offer was that, Mr Elliot?

ELLIOT: My offer to flatter and adore you all the days of your life.

ANNE: I haven't really had a moment, Mr Elliot, to turn my mind to it.

He frowns; she's not normally like this. The BUTLER *opens the door and announces* CAPTAIN HARVILLE *and* CAPTAIN WENTWORTH, *who enter the room and bow to* LADY DALRYMPLE *before approaching* SIR WALTER. ELIZABETH *adopts a coquettish pose for* WENTWORTH's *benefit.*

SIR WALTER: Captain Wentworth! Come in, come in. What will you play? Canasta?

WENTWORTH: Sir Walter, I have come on business.

SIR WALTER: Business?

WENTWORTH: My proposal of marriage has been accepted by your daughter Anne, and I respectfully request permission to fix a date.

SIR WALTER: Anne?

There is surprise amongst the party. ANNE *smiles happily at* WENTWORTH. ELLIOT *is quietly furious.* ELIZABETH's *not exactly thrilled, either.*

SIR WALTER: You want to marry Anne? (*With a glance towards* ELIZABETH): Whatever for?

ELLIOT *catches* MRS CLAY's *eye across the room. She slips out of the door, unnoticed, and he makes a move to follow her.*

CABIN. DAY.

ANNE *sits on a small chair in a small, dark room, writing. Her trunk is on the floor beside her. There is a strange creaking noise all around her. She stands and heads for the door.*

Distantly, we hear a seagull's cry.

STAIRS. DAY.

ANNE *makes her way up a flight of dark, poky stairs.*

WARSHIP. DAY.

ANNE *emerges into blinding sunlight. She comes out of a hatchway on to the deck of a warship under full sail.*

She makes her way across the deck towards the wheel. A burly SAILOR *is standing at it. Behind him are* WENTWORTH, *in command, and his officers. The officers part to allow* ANNE *through. She takes up a position next to* WENTWORTH, *braced against the roll of the ship. He looks briefly at her and smiles. She smiles back, happy beyond belief. She scans the glinting ocean.*

Methuen Modern Plays

include work by

Jean Anouilh
John Arden
Margaretta D'Arcy
Peter Barnes
Sebastian Barry
Brendan Behan
Edward Bond
Bertolt Brecht
Howard Brenton
Simon Burke
Jim Cartwright
Caryl Churchill
Noël Coward
Sarah Daniels
Nick Dear
Shelagh Delaney
David Edgar
Dario Fo
Michael Frayn
John Godber
Paul Godfrey
John Guare
Peter Handke
Jonathan Harvey
Iain Heggie
Declan Hughes
Terry Johnson
Barrie Keeffe
Stephen Lowe
Doug Lucie

John McGrath
David Mamet
Patrick Marber
Arthur Miller
Mtwa, Ngema & Simon
Tom Murphy
Phyllis Nagy
Peter Nichols
Joseph O'Connor
Joe Orton
Louise Page
Joe Penhall
Luigi Pirandello
Stephen Poliakoff
Franca Rame
Philip Ridley
Reginald Rose
David Rudkin
Willy Russell
Jean-Paul Sartre
Sam Shepard
Wole Soyinka
C. P. Taylor
Theatre de Complicite
Theatre Workshop
Sue Townsend
Judy Upton
Timberlake Wertenbaker
Victoria Wood

Methuen World Classics

Aeschylus (two volumes)
Jean Anouilh
John Arden (two volumes)
Arden & D'Arcy
Aristophanes (two volumes)
Aristophanes & Menander
Brendan Behan
Aphra Behn
Edward Bond (four volumes)
Bertolt Brecht
  (five volumes)
Büchner
Bulgakov
Calderón
Anton Chekhov
Noël Coward (five volumes)
Sarah Daniels (two volumes)
Eduardo De Filippo
David Edgar (three volumes)
Euripides (three volumes)
Dario Fo (two volumes)
Michael Frayn (two volumes)
Max Frisch
Gorky
Harley Granville Barker
  (two volumes)
Henrik Ibsen (six volumes)
Terry Johnson
Lorca (three volumes)

Marivaux
Mustapha Matura
David Mercer (two volumes)
Arthur Miller
  (five volumes)
Anthony Minghella
Molière
Tom Murphy
  (three volumes)
Musset
Peter Nichols (two volumes)
Clifford Odets
Joe Orton
Louise Page
A. W. Pinero
Luigi Pirandello
Stephen Poliakoff
  (two volumes)
Terence Rattigan
Ntozake Shange
Sophocles (two volumes)
Wole Soyinka
David Storey (two volumes)
August Strindberg
  (three volumes)
J. M. Synge
Ramón del Valle-Inclán
Frank Wedekind
Oscar Wilde

Methuen Student Editions